John Haiman

Targets and Syntactic Change

JANUA LINGUARUM

STUDIA MEMORIAE
NICOLAI VAN WIJK DEDICATA

edenda curat

C. H. VAN SCHOONEVELD

Indiana University

Series Minor, 186

TARGETS AND SYNTACTIC CHANGE

by

JOHN HAIMAN

Australian National University

Canberra

1974

MOUTON

THE HAGUE · PARIS

LIBRARY OF CONGRESS CATALOG CARD NUMBER: 73-87535

Printed in the Netherlands by ZND, 's-Hertogenbosch

ACKNOWLEDGEMENTS

I would like to express my gratitude to The Canada Council, for a doctoral grant which made possible the writing of this book; and to a large number of informants and teachers, for keeping my blunders down to a hopefully tolerable minimum.

For German data, I am particularly indebted to Mrs. Heidi Rivinus, Mrs. E. Patz, Mrs. F. Moeller, Hans Kuhn, and Erich and Jutta Burgstaller.

For Italian, to Mario del Pozzo.

For Dutch, to F. van Rooseveldt.

For Serbo-Croatian, to Mrs. M. Simic.

For Danish, to Henning Andersen.

For Surselvan Romansh, to U. Candinas and N. Berter.

For other languages with which I am even more unfamiliar, my indebtedness is indicated in the bibliography: but I owe special thanks to S. Anderson for pointing out to me a particularly ghastly blunder in Modern Icelandic, which I made in an earlier version of this study.

For innumerable improvements in exposition, and much good advice on technical points, particularly in part one, I am grateful to Susumu Kuno, and to John Ross.

I owe a large and readily ascertainable debt to my teacher, David Perlmutter, whose investigation of surface structure constraints provided both the inspiration and the point of departure for most of the ideas outlined in part II.

Finally I wish to thank my adviser George Lakoff, to whose encouragement and friendship over the years of my linguistic training I owe much more than this, or any other, acknowledgement could properly indicate.

Canberra   J. H.

TABLE OF CONTENTS

INTRODUCTION

The present work is a synchronic and historical investigation of a most restricted area of German syntax, namely, the position of the verb. Central to this particular treatment is the crucial notion of 'linguistic target', a concept which represents an emendation of the classical theory of transformational generative grammar.

In recent work, it has been amply demonstrated that independently motivated and formally unrelated rules in the grammar of a language may in a sense 'conspire' to produce some kind of favourite surface structure peculiar to that language.

The earliest, and possibly the best-known demonstration of such a conspiracy is that of Kisseberth (1970), in which it is shown that at least six independently motivated phonological rules in the grammar of the Yawelmani dialect of Yokuts recapitulate a morpheme structure condition which prohibits triliteral word-medial, and biliteral word-initial and word-final consonant clusters. Since the publication of this article, a number of other cases of phonological conspiracies have been discussed (Ross, 1970b, Haiman, 1971, 1972), and, by tacit but general agreement, the results of these conspiracies have been designated as TARGETS.

The term 'target' itself is proposed in a much earlier paper (Hoenigswald, 1963), where it is argued that diachronic rather than synchronic processes may be subordinated to a particular goal which may be so described. The idea, however, is probably a good deal older than that. A typical case in point is the observation in Smyth (1956, 18) that Classical Attic Greek avoided two-vowel chains and took steps to eliminate them whether they arose from the collocation of different words, or as the result of derivational or inflectional processes. Here too, as in the discussion of Yawelmani, a number of formally unrelated phonological processes are described together: the criterion for their rapprochement is precisely the fact that there is a single specific job which, in their individual ways, they perform. It is probable that a cursory examination of any competent grammatical description of most languages will reveal similar instances of phonological conspiracies.

In the field of syntax, although targets have been recognized, far more significant work remains to be done than is the case in phonology. It is, for example, a grammatical *cliché* that an expression like the Latin *statua Myronis* (cited in Fillmore 1968) may have a number of different meanings corresponding to as many deep structures. Similarly, it has been pointed out by G. Lakoff (ms.) that to the best of our knowledge, common prenominal determiners like *healthy, many, same, usual* (as in *the usual arguments*) and *utter* (as in *an utter impossibility*) originate in totally different deep structures, and are brought into their common position by a variety of seemingly unrelated rules.

Far more complex examples of systematic constructional ambiguity have been discussed, originally as compelling arguments for the existence of transformational rules. The English surface structure string *NP be Adjective to VP* probably corresponds to more than a dozen possible deep structures, among them the by now notorious *Max is easy to please* and *Max is eager to please* (Lees, 1960; Bolinger, 1961).

Additional examples are easy to adduce. But whereas in phonology, the description of a conspiracy is almost an end in itself, one feels a profound dissatisfaction with merely enumerating apparent surface structure targets in a particular language. The reason for this is twofold. In the first place, phonological targets are quite frequently language specific. The discovery of such a target is not an invitation to speculations about universal grammar. In the second place, those phonological targets which seem to recur, as for example the elimination of vowel chains or of complex consonant clusters, or of successive stressed syllables, can probably be identified, on independent grounds, as phonologically UN-MARKED structures.

In syntax, however, this is not the case. Syntactic targets like *Determiner NP* and *NP + genitive* are found recurring in widely separated and unrelated languages, corresponding in each case to almost exactly the same range of underlying constructions. What this suggests is a common semantic denominator for all of these constructions, one which we are unable to define. And even if it were possible to ignore questions of meaning in a discussion of syntactic targets, it would be impossible to appeal to any independently motivated notion of markedness to explain why some constructions seemed to act like targets, and others did not. For while our understanding of markedness in phonological structures may be quite rudimentary, our understanding of this term with respect to syntactic structures is nil. To the best of our knowledge, there is absolutely NO independently motivated basis for identifying a string *NP be Adjective to VP* as either 'marked' or 'unmarked' with respect to any criterion, or in contrast with any other string.

For these reasons, any discussion of target syntactic structures is bound to be incomplete at least until some understanding of the ways in which meaning can dictate surface structure, is available.

A considerably more superficial syntactic target may, however, be more profitably discussed without reference to the mysteries of semantics. While it seems clear that target syntactic structures cannot be understood in isolation from their meanings, WORD ORDER targets do not seem to be related to any particular feature of meaning.

One of the most obvious and familiar examples of a purely formal constraint on word order is the one which specifies the position of the verb in German. While there are no iron-clad rules in any language, it is probably safe to say that the finite verb in principal clauses of declarative sentences stands second almost entirely independent of meaning and stylistics.

In Part I, I will show that whatever the underlying order of constituents in German may be, the *V*/2 CONSTRAINT in principal clauses must be considered a target in the traditional sense, that is, as the outcome of a conspiracy of two or more transformational rules or conditions.

Part II contains a summary and incomplete examination of the historical development of the $V/2$ constraint in a limited number of Germanic languages. I contend that the surface structure constraint which requires the presence of subject pronouns in the so-called 'type A languages' (Perlmutter, 1968) is a consequence of the $V/2$ constraint, and that, in fact, only those languages which at some stage of their development have been strictly $V/2$ languages ever become strict type A languages.

With the fortunate exception of Icelandic, the correlation between the two constraints has become more or less blurred in all the present type A languages. However, several stages of the process whereby this correlation was lost are directly attested: others can be indirectly inferred. I argue that this process is essentially the same in all the type A languages, and can be understood in terms of one basic principle, which is then suggested as a possible mechanism of linguistic change.

The concluding chapter is no more than a brief recognition of some obvious unanswered questions which remain. A satisfactory explanation for the GENESIS of the $V/2$ constraint in Germanic, and more generally, for that of any target, phonological or syntactic, has yet to be attempted. No more do we have any way to predict what may be called the DOMAIN of a target, that is, the constructions in which it obtains. It will, I hope, become apparent in a number of places throughout this discussion that even in the consideration of a purely formal condition such as the $V/2$ constraint in Germanic, it will be impossible to exclude semantic considerations, as promised. Indeed, though in a very minor way, this work can only furnish further evidence for the inseparability of syntax and semantics.

PART I

THE WORD ORDER CONSTRAINT

V/2 IN GERMAN

We may state the *V*/2 constraint in German in the following way:

(1)   The finite verb occurs as the second constituent imme-
        diately dominated by the *S* node, in the *S* in which it
        occurs.

In most traditional grammars, the few counterexamples are dismissed, more or less as the exceptions that confirm the rule.

Verb-initial order, arising through either ellipsis or subject-verb
inversion, is found in casual colloquial style, but verb-third order
occurs in only the most bookish and pedantic usage, and is probably
rejected in all conversation.

Bearing in mind that exceptions do occur, we may turn to those
common sentence types in which the *V*/2 constraint is satisfied.
A number of superficially contrasting word orders are found in
German. We may distinguish three:

(i) Subject-Verb-Object Order
In German, as in English, it is this word order which is most
commonly encountered, and on the strength of it, Greenberg (1963)
identifies German as an *SVO* language.

(2) (a)   *Sie hat mich tief verletzt.*
           'She wounded me deeply.'
    (b)   *Die Hunde bellen.*
           'The dogs are barking.'
    (c)   *Weder Hans noch Dietrich sind zu Hause.*
           'Neither Hans nor Dietrich are at home.'

(ii) Z-Verb-Subject Order
Some constituent Z other than the subject stands at the head of the
sentence. This constituent may be an adverb, an adjective, a noun
phrase, or a subordinate clause, or a conjunction of two or more
of these, i.e. $[Z \text{ and } Z]_Z$. The finite verb follows, thus remaining
the second constituent immediately dominated by S. The subject
generally follows hard on the verb.

(3) (a) *In Zürich ist es kurz nach 1300 geschrieben worden.*
    (b) *Kurz nach 1300 ist es in Zürich geschrieben worden.*
    (c) *Geschrieben worden ist es in Zürich, kurz nach 1300.*
       'It was written in Zurich shortly after 1300.'
    (d) *Wenn ich ein Vöglein wär' und Flüglein hätt', flög' ich zu*
       dir.
       'If I were a little bird, and had little wings, I would fly
       to you.'

At least formally, (i) and (ii) are identical:

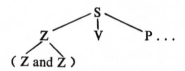

In case (i), Z happens to be equivalent to the subject of the sentence,
while in case (ii), it can be any other constituent but the subject.
While there are unquestionably differences of emphasis and style
between the two, on a purely formal basis there is no reason to
distinguish them.

(iii) es-Verb-Subject Order
This sentence type differs fundamentally from the first two in that
the sentence begins with the semantically neutral particle *es*, which,
unlike the neutre pronoun with which it is morphologically
identical, does not refer to any entity. The verb follows, and is in

turn usually followed by the true subject of the sentence, if such a subject appears in surface structure at all.

(4) (a) *Es kommt der Frühling.*
   'Spring is coming.'

   (b) *Es lebte einmal ein König.*
   'There lived once a king.'

   (c) *Es hat jeder Mensch seine Schwächen.*
   'Everyone has his weaknesses.'

   (d) *Es bellen die Hunde.*
   'The dogs are barking.'

   (e) *Es waren viele Menschen um seine Rettung bemüht.*
   'Many people were concerned about his rescue.'

   (f) *Es schreibt sich gut mit dieser Feder.*
   'It is easy to write with this pen.'

   (g) *Es wurde über das Mädchen gestritten.*
   'The girl was fought over.'

   (h) *Es hat doch jeder Mensch die Bibel einmal gelesen.*
   'Everyone has read the Bible ONCE.'

Sentences of this sort differ in another important way from those in which the initial constituent has some meaning. While there are no substantive limitations on sentences of the form *SVO* or *ZVS*, sentences of type (iii) are rather heavily constrained. Moreover, the judgments of native speakers are widely at variance in assessing the grammaticality of *es*-initial sentences. While most informants agreed on the grammaticality of the utterances of (4), there was considerable disagreement on a number of other similar sentences:

(5) (a) *Es waren meine Eltern um meine Erziehung bemüht.*
   'My parents were concerned about my education.'

   (b) *Es nahmen einige Mädchen Abschied.*
   'Some girls took their leave.'

   (c) *Es kann dem Menschen geholfen werden.*
   'Man can be helped.'

   (d) *Es gab der Mann dem Jungen einen Ball.*
   'The man gave the boy a ball.'

(e)   *Es sehnte sich der Knabe nach Abenteuern.*
      'The boy longed for adventure.'

On the other hand, there was almost unanimous agreement on the utter ungrammaticality of:

(6) (a)   **Es nahmen einige Mädchen einen Apfel.*
           'Some girls took an apple.'
     (b)   **Es hat Hans seine Schwächen.*
           'Hans has his weaknesses.'
     (c)   **Es kann der Mann gesehen werden.*
           'The man can be seen.'
     (d)   **Es hat mein Bruder die Bibel gelesen.*
           'My brother has read the Bible.'
     (e)   **Es sah der Mann die wilde Tiere.*
           'The man saw the wild animals.'
     (f)   **Es kommt er.*
           'He is coming.'

A few general comments on these utterances are in order. To the best of my knowledge, no systematic fullscale attempt has been made to identify the constraints on *es*-initial sentences. It has, however, been often pointed out that they are ungrammatical when the true subject is a personal pronoun. Thus, witness the ungrammaticality of (6f). Beyond this, there seems to be very little of a systematic nature that can be said. There is a general tendency, it is true, to favour generic or indefinite subjects, but witness the acceptability of (4a) and (4d); there is also a tendency to reject sentences in which the main verb is the auxiliary verb *haben* 'have', or the auxiliary or copula *sein* 'be', yet witness the acceptability of (4c) and (4e). A case may be made for the apparent auxiliary *waren* in the latter sentence as an existential verb, in which case, a slightly more abstract representation for (4e) would be:

(4) (e)   *Es waren viele Menschen, die um seine Rettung bemüht waren.*
           'There were many people who were concerned about rescuing him.'

But no similar case could be made for the (almost) equally acceptable (5a).

Our position, fortunately, is this: we need not at the present time concern ourselves with the exact statement of the conditions on *es*-sentences, which is perhaps just as well. We need only note that in these sentences, too, the finite verb is the second constituent to be immediately dominated by the *S* node. Bearing this in mind, we may turn to a preliminary consideration of the STATUS of the introductory particle *es*. If, as we wish to claim, it has no meaning, what is it doing in the sentence at all?

In traditional grammars, introductory *es* is frequently explained as a place-filler, with no other function than that of keeping the verb in second position, in conformity with the *V*/2 constraint. A clear statement of this view may be found in Beneš (1962, 8):

This particle (even though it may be more or less semantically coloured) functions only as an introductory element or 'filler'; it occurs as a place-holder, in order to allow the finite verb to occur as the first communicative element, without thereby destroying its grammatical second position.

Sentences with initial *es* are then described as having 'concealed initial position' of the finite verb. At least two strong arguments can be found in support of this view.

I. OCCURRENCE PRIVILEGES OF THE PARTICLE *ES*

Consider the sentences of (3). In each of these, the dummy *es* is all that keeps the verb from sentence-initial position. Ignoring shifts of emphasis, all of the sentences of (3) can be rewritten with either *ZVS* or *SV*... order. In each case where this is done, however, there will be no room for a dummy *es* anywhere in the sentence:

(7) (a) *Der Frühling kommt(*es)*.
         'Spring is coming.'
     (b) *Ein König lebte (*es) einmal.*
         'Once there lived a king.'

(c) *Jeder Mensch hat (*es) seine Schwächen.*
     'Everybody has his weaknesses.'

From this it follows that if the $V/2$ constraint is satisfied, dummy *es* cannot appear.

However, this constraint does not hold in questions, where the finite verb can occur either initially or in second position, exactly as in English. Not surprisingly, in view of the 'Beneš hypothesis', dummy *es* is never found in questions:

(8) (a) *Wann kommt (*es) der Frühling?*
          'When is spring coming?'
     (b) *Wie schreibt (*es) sich mit dieser Feder?*
          'How does this pen write?'
     (c) *Klingen (*es) die Glocken?*
          'Are the bells ringing?'

Similarly, the constraint does not hold in subordinate clauses, where the verb, whether finite or not, must stand at the end of the clause. Once again, in subordinate clauses, we never find dummy *es*:

(9) (a) *Es ist nicht zu leugnen, dass (*es) jeder Mensch seine Schwächen hat.*
          'It cannot be denied that everyone has his weaknesses.'
     (b) *Sie fragen, ob (*es) viele Menschen um seine Rettung bemüht waren.*
          'They are asking whether many people were concerned about rescuing him.'
     (c) *Solange (*es) die Glocken klingen, bleibt Gummiburg frei.*
          'As long as the bells are ringing, Gummiburg remains free.'

Thus, *es* can appear only where it is needed to satisfy the $V/2$ constraint in those sentences where this constraint holds.

Most of the sentences of (4) have in common the feature that they are somewhat archaic; in most cases, we would encounter rather the sentences of (7), in which it is a meaning-bearing element that occupies initial position. Yet this particle is regularly and ineluctably present in one class of sentences: these are the impersonal passives, typified by (4g), and the following examples:

(10) (a) *Es wird gewalzt.*
       'Steamroller at work.'
  (b) *Es wurde getanzt.*
       'There was dancing.'
  (c) *Es wurde gestritten.*
       'There was fighting.'
  (d) *Es wird gefoltert.*
       'Torture is practised.'

Formally, these sentences are identical to passives derived from active sentences with transitive verbs and direct objects. But a glance at the main verbs in the sentences of (9) suffices to show that the superficial subject *es* cannot in these cases be the object of a corresponding active sentence, for these putative corresponding active sentences are either impossible or do not mean the same as the passives with which they would have to be related:

(11) (a) **Man walzt es.*
       'Steamroller at work.'
  (b) **Man tanzt es.*
       'There is dancing.'
  (c) **Man stritt es.*
       'There was fighting.'
  (d) **Man foltert es.*
       'Torture is practised.'

In the first three, the main verb is intransitive and no direct object is possible; in the last, if the verb has an object, the sentence must refer to some specific creature who is subjected to torture; this is not, however the case in (10d), where merely the activity of torture is described, without reference to any particular victims.

    The existence and structure of impersonal passives pose two problems for us: first, why are they possible at all, and second, why does a dummy subject appear in any of them? Let us postpone the first question (forever, if possible) and attempt an answer to the second. I would wish to claim that *es* appears in (9) for one reason: in these sentences it is the only element which possibly CAN keep the finite verb in second position. For some obscure reason, the following sentences are unacceptable:

(12) (a) *Gewaltzt wird.*
  'Steamroller at work.'
 (b) *Getanzt wurde.*
  'There was dancing.'
 (c) *Gestritten wurde.*
  'There was fighting.'
 (d) *Gefoltert wurde.*
  'Torture was practised.'

But note the consequences:

(a) if the past participle is allowed to carry contrastive stress and stand at the head of the sentence:

(13) (a) *Getanzt wurde (*es) nur in diesem Saal.*
  'There was dancing only in this hall.'
 (b) *Gefoltert wird (*es) nicht nur in Brasilien.*
  'Torture is not practised only in Brazil.'

(b) if some other constituent is available for fronting, and is, in fact, fronted:

(14) (a) *Darüber wurde (*es) gestritten.*
  'There was fighting over that.'
 (b) *Hier wird (*es) gewalzt.*
  'Steamroller at work here.'
 (c) *In Brasilien wird (*es) gefoltert.*
  'Torture is practised in Brazil.'

Moreover, exactly the same situation is observed in questions:

(15) (a) *Wurde (*es) darüber gestritten?*
  'Was there fighting over that?'

(b) *Wurde (*es) gestern Abend getanzt?*
     'Was there dancing last night?'
(c) *Wird (*es) auch in Kanada gefoltert?*
     'Is torture practised in Canada too?'

and, not surprisingly, in subordinate clauses:

(16) (a) *Wer hätte glauben können, dass (*es) auch in Kanada
           gefoltert würde?*
           'Who could have believed that torture would also be
           practised in Canada?'
     (b) *Er fragte, ob (*es) über das Mädchen gestritten wurde.*
           'He asked whether the girl had been fought over.'

That is, the privileges of occurrence for dummy *es* are exactly the
same in impersonal passives as they are in the admittedly somewhat
archaic but structurally analogous sentences of (4).

These facts suggest the following hypotheses: there exists in the
grammar of German a transformational rule of *es*-insertion, which
is constrained in at least two ways: first, it can apply only in those
clauses where the *V*/2 constraint holds, and second, it must be
ordered AFTER rules which front or prepose constituents in the
sentence. Given these constraints, the rule may be stated:

(17) $\# \# \ V \Rightarrow \# \# \ es \ V$

Let us now turn to a more complex and apparently more tenuous
argument in support of this hypothesis.

II. THE DISTINCTION BETWEEN EXISTENCE AND COPULA VERBS

Although the usual idiom to express existence in German is *es gibt*,
under certain circumstances that need not concern us here, *sein*
'to be' can be used as the existential verb. There are syntactic
differences between the existential and the homophonous copula,
relating to the appearance of the dummy pronoun *es*. With few
exceptions (but cf. 5a), the copula cannot occur with sentence-
initial *es:*

(18) (a) *Es ist mein Hund für die Jagd zu alt.
          'My dog is too old for hunting.'
    (b)   *Es ist meine Ruhe hin.
          'My peace (of mind) is gone.'

Existential *sein*, on the other hand, can occur with sentence-initial *es:*

(19) (a) Es ist kein Zweifel, dass etwas schiefgegangen ist.
          'There is no doubt that something has gone awry.'
    (b)   Es sind in diesem Zimmer zwei Stühle.
          'There are two chairs in this room.'
    (c)   Es ist ein Gott im Himmel.
          'There is a God in Heaven.'

And, in fact, it is generally the case that *SVO* order with existential *sein* is impossible:

(20) (a) *Kein Zweifel ist, dass etwas schiefgegangen ist.
          'There is no doubt that something has gone awry.'
    (b)   *Ein Gott ist im Himmel.
          'There is a God in Heaven.'

Usually it is possible, not to say preferable, to front some constituent of the sentence. When this is done, dummy *es* must go; and the same is true in questions and in subordinate clauses:

(21) (a) Im Himmel ist (*es) ein Gott.
          'In Heaven there is a God.'
    (b)   Sind (*es) in diesem Zimmer zwei Stühle?
          'Are there two chairs in this room?'
    (c)   Er fragt, ob (*es) gestern Abend ein Tanz war.
          'He asks whether there was a dance last night.'

That is, existential and copula *sein* are distinguished by the ability of the former to cooccur with sentence-initial *es*. This particle is defined by the same privileges of occurrence that characterize the introductory particle of (3) and the dummy subject of the impersonal passives of (9). Consequently, in those sentences where the

V/2 constraint is satisfied or does not hold, the syntactic opposition between the two homophonous verbs is neutralized.

The question to which we now address ourselves is the nature of this opposition, and how it can be construed as evidence for the transformational origin of introductory *es*.

In the scant literature on targets and rule conspiracies, it is generally contended that there exists a phenomenon that may be schematically represented in the following way:

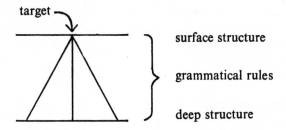

That is, a number of formally dissimilar rules can relate various deep and intermediate structures by mapping them on to one preferred surface structure. It is the common SURFACE configuration that defines both the target and the class of functionally related rules. Another conception of this notion is perfectly possible, however, namely the one that is suggested by the opposite schema:

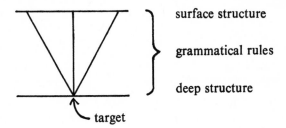

Here, one underlying structure is mapped on to a variety of superficial forms, and qualifies as the target. Functionally related rules

are now defined in terms of their common point of DEPARTURE from the base, rather than their common ARRIVAL in surface structure. It should be recognized that the use of such terms as 'arrival' and 'departure', which imply directionality of derivations, are to be taken purely metaphorically, and are without grammatical significance. Since it is generally agreed that there is no sense in talking about the 'directionality of derivations' in a transformational grammar (cf. Chomsky, 1969; Lakoff, 1969), there is also no reason to restrict the notion of targets to superficial structures only.

Examples of deep structure targets in syntax are numerous. To consider only one, take the semantic representation that we may provisionally represent (following Perlmutter, 1968) as

(22) $[PRO]_{NP}$ VP

It is immediately apparent that structures with this general meaning can be spelled out in a number of ways:

(a) indefinite pronoun + VP

Both French and German have special pronouns, *on* and *man* respectively, that correspond in meaning to *PRO*. English, with no such special pronoun, is forced to make do with the indefinite pronoun *one*, or personal pronouns like *we*, *you*, or *they* used non-referentially. All of these have slightly different privileges of occurrence, and none of them are exactly equivalent in meaning to *PRO*. By way of illustration only, consider the following sets of sentences:

(23) (a)   They say that love is blind.
     (b)   ?We say that love is blind.
     (c)   *You say that love is blind.
     (d)   *One says that love is blind.
(24) (a)   You never can tell with hephalumps.
     (b)   *They never can tell with hephalumps.
     (c)   ?We never can tell with hephalumps.
     (d)   One never can tell with hephalumps.
(25) (a)   We generally designate this curve as a parabola.
     (b)   *They generally designate this curve as a parabola.

(c)   *You generally designate this curve as a parabola.

(d)   One generally designates this curve as a parabola.

The same is superficially true of languages like Russian, where the third person plural form of the verb suggests a deleted third person plural subject, the pronoun *oni* 'they'. But although Russian allows subject pronoun deletion in general without change of meaning, this is not the case with examples like:

(26) (a)   *oni govor'at*   they$_1$ say

     (b)   *govor'at*   they$_2$ say

which do not mean the same thing. Of these forms, the latter is ambiguous: the subject may be either a definite group of people known to the speaker and/or the listener, or the indefinite agent *PRO*. On the other hand, (26a) is unambiguous: the subject can only be a definite group of people.

Of the two meanings of (26b), only one can be the result of the deletion of the definite pronoun *oni*, and this is not the meaning with a *PRO* subject. This suggests to me that Russian, like French and German, has a distinct indefinite pronoun, just like French and German, but that this pronoun, unlike French *on* and German *man*, is never spelled out in surface structure. Although I am not certain of this, I would suspect that the same is true of languages like Italian with the contrast *Loro dicono* 'they say' and *dicono* 'they say'.

(b) Nominalization of verb + existential verb

This construction is attested in English, and in at least one unrelated language, Hungarian:

(27) (a)   There was dancing in the streets.

     (b)   *Volt táncolás.* (= 'was dancing')

(c) Impersonal passives

As we have seen, this construction is represented in German (10). The same is true in at least two more languages where no subject pronoun is found, Latin and Turkish:

(28) (a)   *Pugnat-ur.*
         fight (3sg. pres.) + passive
         'There is fighting.'
    (b) *Döv-   üş-   ül-   dü.*
         hit   (reciprocal) (passive) (past 3 sg.)
         'There was fighting.'

(d) Impersonal reflexives

These are found to occur freely in at least one language known to me, Serbo-Croatian, and are subject to varying limitations in other languages like Russian, French, and German.

(29) (a) *Doma n'e s'id'it- s'a v vos'emnadcat' l'et.*   (Russian)
         at-home not sit (refl.) at eighteen years
         'One $\begin{Bmatrix} \text{can} \\ \text{does} \end{Bmatrix}$ not sit at home when one is eighteen.'
    (b) *Plesa   se.*   (S.-C.)
         dance (3sg.)   refl.
         'There is dancing.'
    (c) *Ça se voit*
         'One can see that.'   'That is obvious.'
    (d) *Es fragt sich, ob...*
         'One wonders whether...'

With the exception of the indefinite noun phrase + *VP* construction, none of these bears any close structural similarity to the underlying representation from which it is presumably derived. The fact that these four surface structures (among others, no doubt) recur in diverse languages is probably no accident, but certainly a mystery in the light of our present knowledge about grammatical processes such as the passive and reflexive transformations. It is consequently a weakness in grammatical theory as presently understood that the intuitively perceived connections between these rules are not formally characterized in some independent fashion.

   Such an intuitively obvious connection is even more marked in an example directly relevant to the present study, namely the realization of the opposition between the copula and the morphologically identical existential verb in a number of unrelated languages.

Like German and English, a large number of languages have homonymous copula and existential verbs. Like these two, they generally manage to distinguish the two in some way, and although the means whereby a distinction is effected may vary, there is a clearly defined similarity among them which may perhaps be illustrated by a small number of examples.

(i) In Attic Greek, both the copula and the existential verb are rendered by the same verb *eimi*. But there are important differences. In the present indicative, the copula, with the exception of the second person singular *eî*, is invariably atonic: like all bisyllabic clitics, it is stressed on the last syllable, and loses this stress unless it is immediately preceded by a paroxytone or another clitic (Smyth, 1956, 42). Furthermore, it is very frequently deleted altogether:

(30) (a) *He:* *eudaimonía* *enérgeia*
the (fem. sg. nom.) happiness activity
   tis *estín.*
some (-neutre sg. nom.) is
'Happiness is an activity.'

(b) *Toîs* *órnisi*
the (-fem. pl. dat.) birds (masc. dat.)
oux *hoi* *autoí*
not the (masc. pl. nom.) same (masc. pl. nom.)
eisi *nómoi* *hoíper*
are laws (masc. nom.) as they (masc. pl. nom.)
   toîs *állois*
the (-fem. pl. dat.) other (-fem. pl. dat.)
   dzo:íois.
animals (neutre pl. dat.)
'Birds are not subject to the same laws as other creatures.'

(c) *Ho* *bíos*
the (masc. sg. nom.) life (masc. nom.)
   braxús *he:*
short (masc. sg. nom.) the (fem. sg. nom.)

> *de*   *téxne:*
> (adversative particle)   art (fem. nom.)
>   *makré:.*
> long (fem. sg. nom.)
> 'Life is short, art is long.'

(d)   *Hoi*   *pleîstoi*
the (masc. pl. nom.)   most (masc. pl. nom.)
     kakoí.
bad (masc. pl. nom.)
'Most men are bad.'

This is not the case when the copula is emphasised. When this happens, the copula bears normal recessive stress, like any other verb:

(31)   *Ei   éstin   hoúto:s...*
       if   is   thus
       'If it IS so...'

Nor is it the case under a handful of other conditions, summarized in a standard handbook as follows:

estí is written *ésti* at the beginning of a sentence, when it expresses existence or possibility, and when it follows *ouk* 'not' *me:* 'not', *ei* 'if', *ho:s* 'as' *kái* 'and' *allá* 'but', and *toûto* 'this'. (Smyth, 1956, 43).

It is evident that four of these positions, namely following the conjunctions *ei*, *ho:s*, *kái*, and *allá*, are equivalent to clause-initial position. This allows us to reduce the examples of tonic *ésti* to three classes:

(a) after the negative particles and *toûto*
(b) in clause-initial position
(c) as verbs of existence and possibility

Although the syntax of these particles deserves a more detailed investigation than I am qualified to undertake, there seems to be a fairly close correlation between (b) and (c): that is, I have found no examples of clause-initial *ésti* in which the verb did not, in fact, express existence:

(32) (a) *Ésti   mou...*
     is   1 sg. gen.
     'I have...'

(b) *Éstin   hoi...*
     is   they (masc. pl. nom.)
     'There are some who...'

And in fact, there seems to be the same correlation even between (a) and (c), at least in the limited number of cases I have been able to find:

(33) (a) *Ouk   ésti.*
     not   is
     'He is no more.'

(b)   *Anarxías   de*
     anarchy (fem. gen.)   (adversative particle)
       meîdzon   ouk   ésti
     greater (neutre sg. nom.)   not   is
       kakón.
     evil (neutre sg. nom.)
     'There is no evil worse than anarchy.'

Regardless of the behaviour of the verb in the environment of the lexical items enumerated in Smyth's study, a systematic behaviour is always found when the verb means existence, in which case it is never deleted, nor does it take clitic accentuation:

(34) *hóti   men   oûn   éstin   ho*
     that   (particle)   therefore   is   the (masc. sg. nom.)
      tópos   dokeî   dê:lon
     space (masc. nom.)   seems   clear (neutre sg. nom.)
     eînai
     to be
     'That space exists seems to be evident.'

Thus, even though Classical Attic Greek has the same lexical items doing duty for the copula and the existential verb, they are distinguished through accentuation. Significantly, the latter is like the stressed form of the former.

(ii) In modern Russian, the copula and the existential verb are both represented by the verb *bit'* 'to be'. At least in the present indicative, they are distinguished by means of a syntactic rule: the copula is regularly deleted, except in statements of permanent validity (definitions), and when under special stress:

(35) (a) *Abram   gluboko   svoi   par'en'.*
       Abram   deeply   his-own   (m.sg. nom.) fellow
       'Abram's a regular guy.'

(b) *Gd'e   zhe   koshka?*
      where   (particle)   cat (fem. sg. nom.)
      'Where's the cat?'

In statements of permanent validity:

(36) *Kap'ital'izm   jest'   ekonom'icheskaya   s'ist'ema.*
      capitalism   is   economic (fem. sg. nom.)   system
      'Capitalism is an economic system.'

Under special stress:

(37) *Ol'ga   dumajet   chto   ona   kras'iv'eje   chem   ona   jest'.*
      Olga   thinks   that   she   prettier   than   she   is
      'Olga thinks that she is prettier than she is.'

The existential verb, on the other hand, cannot generally be deleted unless a locative phrase is fronted in the sentence in which it occurs:

(38) (a) *U   n'ego   jest'   d'eng'i.*
       at   him (gen. sg. masc.)   is   money
       'He has money.'

(38) (b) *Kolbasa   jest'?*
      sausage   is
      'Is there (any) sausage?'

With a fronted locative predicate phrase, for unknown reasons, the verb is deleted:

(39)   *Na stol'e*   *kn'iga.*
          on table (prepositional)   book
          'On the table there is a book.'

(iii) In Hungarian, the copula and the existential verb are both *lenni* 'to be', but the third person singular and plural of the copula are regularly deleted in the present indicative:

(40)   *Az   uj   császár   nem   olyan   gonosz*
         the   new   emperor   not   so   wicked
         mint   a   régi.
          as   the   former
         'The new emperor is not so wicked as the old.'

However, when the copula is stressed, it cannot be deleted:

(41)   *Az   uj   császár   van   olyan   gonosz*
         the   new   emperor   is   so   wicked
         mint   a   régi.
          as   the   former
         'The new emperor is too as wicked as the old.'

The same is true of the existential verb. Moreover, unlike the copula, it is frequently, as in Greek, the first constituent of the sentence in which it appears:

(42) (a) *Volt   egy   király   Zuzmara.*
          was   a   king   hoar-frost
          'There was (once) a king (called) Hoar-frost.'
     (b) *Vannak   barát-   a-   i   ∅*
          are (3 pl.) friend   (possessive) (plural)   (3 sg.)
          'He has friends.'

At this point, a limited but fairly clear generalization should become apparent. The copula verb may appear in either of two forms, depending on whether or not it is marked for prominence. A difference in prominence may be marked in three distinct but intuitively related ways:

(43)   *+prominent*   *−prominent*
   (a)   initial position   internal position
   (b)   normal stress   clitic stress (= no stress)
   (c)   non-deletability   deletability

In a properly constructed grammatical theory, we should wish to formally recognize the unity of these three superficial oppositions, which reflect a single underlying distinction: in this sense, the basic opposition [$\pm$ *prominent*] may be conceived of as a deep structure target, which is realized in various ways.

It is true that usage of the term presupposes an exact understanding of what PROMINENCE may be, and the conditions under which it may or may not be a feature of particular words. We have no such understanding at the present time: unfortunately, our discussion must depend on widely shared intuitions on what constitutes prominence.

The existential verb *to be*, where it is morphologically identical to the copula, is spelled out as the PROMINENT form of the copula: that is, it will be distinguished by sentence-initial position, or non-deletability, or by orthotonic stress, as the case may be. This is scarcely surprising: under normal conditions, the copula is a purely grammatical cipher, almost totally devoid of semantic content. Consequently, it may be reduced in various ways, unless, of course, it is marked for prominence. The existential verb, on the other hand, is a verb like any other, and hence not generally subject to reduction or deletion.

Insofar as it can be recognized that (42a-c) constitute a unified class of oppositions, related by one common underlying relation, we can state a generalization about homophonous copulas and existential verbs, whose validity extends far beyond the present sample:

(44)   The existential verb will be syntactically identical to the prominent form of the homophonous copula.

But it does not seem that this generalization can apply in German, or the Germanic languages in general. In these languages, without exception, when the two verbs are distinguished at all, it is by means of a sentence-initial semantically empty particle: *es* in German, *there* in English, *er* in Dutch, *það* in Icelandic, and so on. Moreover, as we have seen in German at least, this difference subsists only in declarative sentences, in principal clauses: where the *V*/2 constraint applies. Further, it vanishes even in these sentences if fronting applies to some other constituent in the sentence.

Now there is no intuitively obvious way in which the presence of this particle realizes underlying prominence, nor is it generally associated with any part of speech but the finite verb. Apparently, we can not proceed very far with (44) before stumbling on a systematic class of counterexamples. Yet a modified version of this generalization can be upheld, given two structural features of German.

The first is that prominence in German is frequently realized by sentence-initial position: there is in fact a fronting rule, illustrated by the sentences (2), whose function is to put prominent constituents into this position.

The second is that in German there is a purely mechanical constraint on the position of the verb in declarative sentences: it cannot stand at the head of the sentence.

From these two features, it follows that the behaviour of German may not be deviant with respect to (44) at all. Rather, given the structural limitations imposed on German by the *V*/2 constraint, the difference between existential and copular *sein* is realized by (43a), a difference in word order.

To see how this is so, let us consider two contrasting word orders at a late stage in the derivation of declarative sentences:

(a) $\# \# V ...$
(b) $\# \# Z \ V ...$

This contrast may be regarded in two ways: it may be that fronting can apply to VERBS, in which case the verb in (a) is marked PROMINENT, with no further questions asked; or it may be the case that fronting can not apply to verbs, only other constituents. In this case, the verb in (a) is in initial position because it started there (as would be the case, say, if German were an underlying verb-initial language), and there is no element of (a) which can be designated as PROMINENT.

Even so, there would be a distinction in prominence between the verbs in (a) and (b): sentence-initial position will always be connected with prominence, and a verb that occurs in this position will be marked for this feature, *ipso facto*, with respect to another verb in sentence-internal position.

Now let us assume that both (a) and (b) correspond to German sentences at a stage in the derivation that follows fronting: then the first corresponds to sentences with existential verbs, and the second to sentences with copula verbs.

In surface structure, sentences like (a) are not allowed to exist as declarative sentences, by virtue of the $V/2$ constraint. Hence the word order opposition is nullified in these sentences only, by the operation of a low level rule (17), the proposed rule of *es*-insertion.

We have now shown that if *es*-insertion is indeed regarded as a low-level transformational rule, then it may be possible to extend the validity of (44) to the Germanic languages. Insofar as this is a worthwhile goal, we may regard this as evidence for our proposed analysis of introductory *es*.

Yet clearly, if (44) is to apply to German, it will be in need of certain revision. For although prominence is often reflected through sentence-initial position in German, the stressed or prominent form of the copula is never found occurring with initial *es:* in fact, there is considerable evidence that the copula in German can never occur with dummy *es* under any circumstances (cf. (18)).

Let us then revise our tentative statement of the opposition between the existential verb and its homophone:

(45)   In any language, the existential verb may be marked PROMINENT with respect to the homophonous copula by means of one of the devices in the language whereby prominence is reflected.

At this stage, we provisionally accept the existence of a transformational rule of *es*-insertion in German, and turn our attention
to the central problem of describing a derivation for German
sentences. The contention that we now seek to justify is that the
V/2 constraint will demand for its satisfaction at least two other
conditions besides the existence of a rule of *es*-insertion, and hence
that it is to be described as a target.

The base component of a transformational grammar of German
is totally indeterminate, at least with reference to the order of
constituents, a fact which highlights a crucial and often noted
failing of generative syntax. (cf. Peters and Ritchie, 1969; Peters,
1970). Specifically, given the surface structure orders that appear
in German sentences of various types, it is possible to construct
equally plausible derivations for these sentences which proceed
from any one of three given bases: *SOV* (as in subordinate clauses),
SVO (as in declarative sentences), and *VSO* (as in questions). In
fact, this has already been done by three different investigators,
each of them working within a framework, and accepting the
traditional assumptions of generative grammar.

The status of the *V*/2 constraint will remain unaffected by the
derivation that is adopted as the 'correct' one. Although we will
be concerned mainly with the illustration of this point, I hope to
present some evidence against the *SOV* hypothesis, and a simplicity
argument in favour of the *VSO* hypothesis.

(i) The Bach Hypothesis: SOV order

In one of the earliest transformational analyses of German, Bach
(1962) proposed that a dummy node $\emptyset$ should be generated by the
phrase structure rules. The underlying order of constituents would
then be something like $S\ O\ \emptyset\ V$, with the verb originating in
sentence-final position. Leaving irrelevant details aside, his derivation of German sentences would include:

(a) an optional FRONTING rule that preposes any constituent including $\emptyset$. (The verb, however, is only to be fronted in yes-no questions.)

(b)   an obligatory rule of question formation, triggered by the presence of a sentence-initial Q morpheme, which puts a w-morpheme at the head of the sentence.

(c)   various spelling rules that define the form of the w-morpheme under various conditions, i.e.

$$\# \# \text{ w- } V \qquad \rightarrow \# \# \ V$$
$$\# \# \text{ w- some time } \rightarrow \# \# \ \text{wann}$$
$$\# \# \text{ w- some place } \rightarrow \# \# \ \overline{\text{wo}}$$

and so on.

(d)   various unspecified embedding transformations for subordinate clauses

(e)   an obligatory rule of $V/2$ placement, which moves the NON-fronted verb in principal clauses into second position (i.e., the rule does not apply in questions where it is the verb that has been fronted; it does, however, apply in questions where a question word like *wo, wann, wer* 'who' is the fronted element).

(f)   finally, a spelling rule analogous to (16), which converts $\emptyset$ to *es* in sentence-initial position:

(46) $\# \# \ \emptyset \ V \rightarrow \# \# \ \text{es}, \ V$

Otherwise $\emptyset$ remains, in every sense of the word, null. A typical derivation for an *es*-sentence would then be:

(47)   jeder Mensch seine Schwächen $\emptyset$ hat $(S \ O \ \emptyset \ V) \Rightarrow$
$\emptyset$ jeder Mensch seine Schwächen hat (fronting of $\emptyset$) $\Rightarrow$
$\emptyset$ hat jeder Mensch seine Schwächen $(V/2$ shift) $\Rightarrow$
es hat jeder Mensch seine Schwächen $(\emptyset \Rightarrow \text{es})$

The Bach hypothesis was originally attractive for a number of reasons: first, in identifying German as an underlying SOV language, thereby bringing it closer to those other Indo-European languages such as Latin and Sanskrit, in which superficial verb-final

order is the most commonly occurring type; second, in attempting
to predict the position of the verb in all sentence types by means
of only one rule that had to apply specifically to verbs: finally, in
making the intuitively correct claim that *es*-insertion sentences
were those in which NO fronting-topicalization had occurred – for
what else could be the significance, stylistically, of fronting the
dummy symbol $\emptyset$?

It is on the third point that the validity of the Bach hypothesis
can be most seriously questioned, for it is clear that this hypothesis
distinguishes between those cases where fronting of any sort has
failed to apply (in which case, the superficial order of constituents,
after *V*/2 shift, is *SVO*), and those cases where it applies to the
dummy symbol $\emptyset$ (in which case the final order of constituents
is *es V SO*). And this distinction raises a host of mechanical and
semantic difficulties.

In the first place, it is necessary to question the status of any
dummy node $\emptyset$ in any deep structure, however conceived. Where
does this node appear? What are its syntactic relations of precedence,
dominance, and so on, to other nodes in the sentence? It is impossible to give any meaningful answer to these questions: $\emptyset$ is an
artifact in deep structure: its relation to other elements in the
sentence in which it occurs is totally arbitrary, until it is spelled out
in surface structure as sentence-initial *es*.

Related to this objection is the problem of fronting $\emptyset$. There
seem to be two kinds of fronting in German, and neither of them
is meaningless.

The first of these seems to be related to prominence, as we have
already noted. The fronted constituent is brought to the head of
the sentence because it bears special emphasis of some sort:

(48) (a) *Ihm werde ich kein Geld pumpen.*
          'HIM I won't lend any money to.'
     (b) *So war es nicht gemeint.*
          'It wasn't meant in THAT way.'

The second, or RESUMPTIVE, topicalization is found only in con-
tinuous discourse contexts. The first word of the sentence, usually

an adverb of consecutivity or of consequence, refers back to the time or the action of some previous utterance or set of utterances, and thus acts as a sort of anchor for the sentence in which it appears:

(49) (a) *Da öffnete sich ein zweites Tor.*
          'Then a second door opened.'
     (b) *So ist er zu spät gekommen.*
          'So he arrived late.'

This kind of topicalization is compatible with the Pragian concept of functional sentence perspective: each utterance consists of old and new information, and the tendency is to put old information at the beginning of the sentence, and new information after (cf. Garvin, 1963; Kuno, 1971).

It is clear, however, that $\emptyset$ does not qualify for fronting on either count. Certainly, $\emptyset$ cannot possibly be said to bear any special stress, so it cannot be subject to the first fronting rule; equally evident is the fact that it does not resume old information. In fact, in texts which I have examined, I have found that *es*-sentences occur with the greatest frequency in independent utterances, and as the initiatory sentences of narratives or descriptions. All these, of course, are situations in which resumptive topicalization is impossible, simply because there is nothing to be resumed.

For these reasons, $\emptyset$ fronting is an implausible rule, and insofar as it is, the *SOV* hypothesis is questionable.

(ii) The Ross hypothesis: SVO order

In a paper on Gapping, Ross (1970a) argued against *SOV* in German, and proposed that the underlying order of constituents was *SVO*. He justified his position by a fairly complex argument, having to do with the conditions under which identical-verb deletion could take place in various languages, to relate sentences such as these:

(50) (a)   Bill kicked Sam, and Max kicked Harry.
   (b)   Bill kicked Sam, and Max, Harry.
   (c)   *Bill, Sam, and Max kicked Harry. (grammatical, but not
         synonymous with (a) and (b))

Ross held the view that although true verb-final languages would
permit sentences like (50c), they would never under any circumstances permit forward gapping, as in (50b). Yet German, even
with superficial verb-final order, as in subordinate clauses, allows
BOTH types of gapping to occur:

(51) (a)   *...weil Max ein Narr ist, und Moritz ein Esel ist.*
   (b)   *...weil Max ein Narr ist, und Moritz ein Esel.*
   (c)   *...weil Max ein Narr, und Moritz ein Esel ist.*
         '...because Max is a fool, and Moritz an ass.'

It is not our purpose to evaluate the merits of this argument here,
but note that even if it were to prove absolutely unexceptionable,
it would not prove that German has underlying *SVO* order. The
gapping argument purports only to prove that German cannot
possibly have verb-final order – either *SVO* or *VSO* are compatible
with its contentions, however.

The same is true of a more recent paper by Bach (1971), in which
it is argued that German cannot, as he originally suggested, have
verb-final order. Indeed, in this paper, Bach claims that only two
underlying orders are possible – *VSO* and *SOV* – and contends
that German has the former. Again, it is unnecessary to recapitulate
his arguments at any length, since our main concern is not to
support or to attack the position that they defend, but rather to
demonstrate that regardless of the basic order which we adopt, the
status of the *V*/2 constraint is unaffected.

Yet we must recognize that the *SVO* position is now without
defenders: ironically, in view of the fact that this order is the one
most frequently encountered in declarative sentences. Partly for
this reason, and partly because I believe that there are other
arguments (to be given later) for *SVO*, I will include a sample
derivation for *SVO* sentences.

The chief feature of such a derivation is an otherwise unnecessary rule of subject-verb inversion, which is absolutely indispensable to derive sentences such as (4), with *ZVS* order: that is, subject-verb inversion must follow fronting:

(52) (a) *Es ist in Zürich geschrieben worden.*
  (b) *Geschrieben worden es ist in Zürich.* (fronting)
  (c) *Geschrieben worden ist es in Zürich.* (inversion)
    'It was written in Zürich.'

Given the existence of such a rule, we now have two possible derivations for *es*-sentences, which we may schematically reproduce:

(53)   I   II
  SVO   *SVO*
  es SVO (*es*-insertion)   *VSO* (inversion)
  es VSO (inversion)   *es VSO* (*es*-insertion)

In view of the nature of the evidence that we have presented about the nature of *es*-insertion, we may reject the first of these; there remains the problem of accounting for the application of such a rule as subject-verb inversion in II: if, as we wish to claim, subject-verb inversion exists to keep the verb in second position after fronting, why does it apply at all in *es*-sentences? Although both derivations of (53) will work, they both seem to be intuitively wrong in some way: if both *es*-insertion and subject-verb inversion are included in the grammar of German in order to keep the verb in second position, there is no reason for either of them to apply, given an *SVO* base, and the existence of *es*-sentences constitutes a real problem for the *SVO* hypothesis.

(iii) The McCawley hypothesis: VSO order

Using arguments of a purely formal nature, McCawley (1970) has urged that English be considered a *VSO* language. So divorced from empirical considerations are these arguments that their cogency is undiminished in German, or, indeed, in any other

superficial *SVO* language where rules such as the passive transformation operate roughly as they do in English. Once again, we
may dispense with any recapitulation of these arguments, as they
are irrelevant to our present discussion.

But assumption of verb-initial order will yield a great simplifica-
tion in our derivation of German sentences as well as providing the
only natural explanation for *es-VSO*-sentences.

A fronting rule will permit any constituent, INCLUDING THE
SUBJECT, to precede the verb. If this rule applies, all is well and the
derivation is complete; if it does not, a subsequent rule of *es*-
insertion must apply to keep the verb in second position.

This version of the McCawley hypothesis embodies the oft-
repeated truism that the topic of a sentence is usually the subject,
at least in Indo-European languages. The canonical order of constituents is then the consequence not of underlying *SVO* order, but
rather of the fronting rule, and it is the canonical order simply
because the fronting rule, in the unmarked case, applies to subjects.

According to this analysis, *es*-sentences are then those in which
fronting has simply failed to occur. If we equate fronting with
topicalization, this is more or less what we should expect. As noted,
these sentences occur frequently as initial or independent utterances,
in which all the information conveyed is equally new and equally
important. Hence the preponderance of these sentences as the
initiators of discourse provides some (admittedly weak) evidence
for the appropriateness of a *VSO* analysis.

Nevertheless it is plain that we cannot uncritically equate
FRONTING with TOPICALIZATION in German (or, for that matter in
English, where the facts are essentially the same). There are only
too many examples of *SVO* order in both languages where the
topic-comment distinction does not correspond to the subject-
predicate distinction at all:

(54) (a)   Only Max eats peas.
     (b)   Who came?
     (c)   A woman's voice broke the silence.

In each of these, it seems to be the predicate phrase which acts as

the topic, or which, roughly speaking, resumes the known information, while the subject noun phrase is the comment, or, alternatively,
the focus, in which new information is either requested or supplied.

In essence, both our version of the McCawley hypothesis and
the problems involved with equating fronting and topicalization
were noted in Curme's classic *Syntax* (Curme, 1931, 351), where it is
proposed that

Originally the normal word order, i.e. the subject in first place, was
identical with the inverted word order, that is, the subject stood in the
first place for emphasis, or to establish a relation with what preceded
it. THIS IS NOT NOW ITS USUAL FORCE...

In the absence of detailed evidence on the nature of topicalization
in old English or German, this claim can only be regarded as
suggestive. We do, however, hope to present some arguments for
its validity in the following chapter.

Before leaving this problem for the present, I would like to
illustrate one respect in which topicalization and subject position
are related even in present day English.

It has been pointed out to me (S. Kuno; personal communication) that indefinite noun phrases (as opposed to generics) usually
cannot serve as the topics of sentences. Nevertheless, as we can see
from (54c) and countless other examples, indefinite noun phrases
can serve as the SUBJECTS of grammatical sentences.

But Perlmutter (1970) has shown that sentences with indefinite
subjects are subject to heavy constraints. As illustration, we may
cite the following English sentences, which are all, like their
German counterparts, deviant in some way:

(55) (a)   A clown looked perplexed.
     (b)   A horse breathed deeply.
     (c)   A butler scratched his wrist.
     (d)   A co-ed glanced at her navel.
     (e)   A cardinal sat down.

For our own limited purposes, it is sufficient to note that all of
these sentences become perfectly normal and unexceptionable when

the subjects are definite, as in:

(56) (a)   The clown looked perplexed.
   (b)   The horse breathed deeply.
   (c)   The butler scratched his wrist.
   (d)   The co-ed glanced at her navel.
   (e)   The cardinal sat down.

Thus, at least for this class of examples, only possible topic noun phrases can serve as subjects.

A slightly more lingering investigation will reveal the perfect grammaticality of other sentences with indefinite subjects:

(57) (a)   A clown set off the firecrackers.
   (b)   A horse whinnied.
   (c)   A butler dragged the hippy off to the coal cellar.
   (d)   A co-ed screamed an unprintable obscenity at him.
   (e)   A cardinal intoned the De Profundis.

I suspect that the relative acceptability of these sentences, in contrast to those of (55), depends at least in part on a factor that most people would unhesitatingly designate as extralinguistic: this is the degree of NOTICEABILITY of the action described in the predicate phrase. When the action is relatively unobtrusive, as is the case with *looking perplexed*, *breathing gently*, and the like, it seems that no subject of an indefinite nature is possible. On the other hand, if the action is (preferably blatantly) obvious, as is the case with *whinnying*, *screaming obscenities*, and their ilk, indefinite subjects are possible.

At first glance, this may seem to be a totally arbitrary and inexplicable correlation. In fact, however, it can be related in an intuitively satisfying, though at present unformalizable way with the topic-comment distinction.

Roughly speaking, a topic contains information which is already known, or which for some reason, does not need to be pointed out anew. A blatantly obvious action will presumably qualify as a possible topic: this is in fact the case in the sentences of (57). We can already HEAR the firecrackers: the new information, or comment, is that it was a clown that set them off. And the same kind of analysis is possible for all the other sentences in this group.

This is not so with the sentences of (55). Unless we already have our attention directed to someone, we will not notice that he looks perplexed; nor will we observe any of the other unobtrusive actions described in these sentences, unless we have previously been told who to look at or what to look for.

I suggest that the sentences of (55) are deviant because no element within them suggests itself as a possible topic – they are ALL COMMENT; all of the sentences of (57), however, are grammatical, because the clearly defined and evident actions therein described can function as topics.

Let me emphasize that the foregoing can only be considered the crudest approximation to the truth, and that a number of other factors will doubtless enter into the consideration of all these sentences. Then we may provisionally state the following constraint on English sentences:

(58)   Sentences with indefinite subjects are fully permissible only if their predicates qualify as possible topics.

Our claim is that (54) are ungrammatical, or at least, deviant, because they lack topics.

Moreover, our claim is that in German, *es-VSO*-sentences also lack topics. In support of this we may say first that the vast majority of *es*-sentences in German, though not, unfortunately, all of them, have indefinite subjects. This fact is explained if we equate topicalization with fronting: in *es*-sentences, no fronting has occurred, since the subject, being indefinite, is not eligible for the status of TOPIC.

We therefore claim that topicless sentences can and do occur in German, and that they are frequently *es*-sentences. We are consequently forced to make certain predictions about the German equivalents of (55): that they will be deviant, as are their English counterparts, with *SVO*-order, but since their ungrammaticality is the result of FRONTING noun phrases which cannot possibly be topics, they will be acceptable if fronting does not occur. That is, we predict that as *es*-sentences, they will be acceptable.

This prediction, which, if confirmed, would provide dazzling support for our hypothesis, unfortunately fails to materialize. As predicted, the German translations of (55) are indeed deviant:

(59) (a)   *Ein Clown sah verlegen drein.*
   (b)   *Ein Pferd atmete tief.*
   (c)   *Ein Diener kratzte sich am Handgelenk.*
   (d)   *Eine Studentin warf einen Blick auf ihren Nabel.*
   (e)   *Ein Kardinal setzte sich.*

and, furthermore, they are acceptable with definite subjects. But the *es*-sentences corresponding to (59) are not better but rather worse than these sentences:

(60) (a)   **Es sah ein Clown verlegen drein.*
   (b)   **Es atmete tief ein Pferd.*
   (c)   **Es kratzte sich ein Diener am Handgelenk.*
   (d)   **Es warf eine Studentin einen Blick auf ihren Nabel.*
   (e)   **Es setzte sich ein Kardinal.*

The reason, it has been suggested (H. Kuhn, personal communication) is that *es*-insertion may generally take place with only a small class of verbs of a rather colourless nature, and that none of the actions described above is sufficiently GENERAL and neutral to allow *es*-insertion. An investigation of this claim is not pursued here, for once again, the judgments of native speakers are widely at variance in assessing the grammaticality of these sentences: some people will find (60) perfectly acceptable, but by and large, they will be the same people who do not find (59) in any way deviant.

But even if the results were everything that we could wish, our hypothesis that FRONTING = TOPICALIZATION would still not have been confirmed. There are far too many examples of *SVO*-order in both German and English that do not correspond to TOPIC + COMMENT order. At best, we can say only that there exists between the two an obscure but still perceptible correlation that may or may not at one time have been more general.

For the remainder of the present discussion, we will abandon the usage of the term TOPICALIZATION, and use the term FRONTING to refer to the purely mechanical process that shifts constituents to the beginning of the sentence in which they appear. We are now in a position to demonstrate that:

(a) Regardless of the underlying order of constituents in German, the $V/2$ constraint presses into its service a number of formally related rules and conditions on their application.
(b) That if simplicity of derivations is a criterion, the VSO-base is to be preferred for the derivation of German sentences.

If the order of constituents is SOV, the $V/2$ constraint follows from the existence of the following necessary conditions on derivations:

(i)   A terminal dummy element $\emptyset$ must be generated by the phrase structure rules, and must be available for fronting.
(ii) The existence of a fronting rule.
(iii) The verb-shift rule in declarative sentences.
(iv) The spelling rule $\emptyset \rightarrow es$.

If the underlying order of constituents is SVO, there must exist a more complex battery of conditions:

(i)   The base order SVO, in which the verb is already found in second position.
(ii) A rule of subject-verb-inversion.
(iii) An ordering constraint which states that (ii) must apply after fronting.
(iv) A rule of es-insertion.
(v)   An ordering constraint that states the relation of (ii) and (iv): that (iv) applies after (ii).

Note that in this derivation, for all its complexity, the derivation merely recapitulates a constraint which is already satisfied in deep structure. This is not true of the other derivations.

If the underlying order is VSO, the $V/2$ constraint is satisfied by the interaction of:

(i)   Fronting.

(ii) *Es*-insertion.

(iii) The condition that in any sentence, either (i) or (ii) but not both may apply.

It is now clear that *VSO* is the simplest base from which to derive *ZV*... and *es V*... sentences, but that in any case the derivation of these sentences, both satisfying the *V*/2 constraint, requires a relation of several rules.

(61)   German is a *VSO* language.

(62)   The *V*/2 constraint is a target.

SURFACE STRUCTURE CONDITIONS

It is the aim of this chapter to forestall the plausible and quite sensible objection that the $V/2$ constraint should be regarded not as a TARGET, the outcome of a rule conspiracy but rather as a SURFACE STRUCTURE CONDITION, a constraint imposed on terminal sentences, independently of the transformational rules involved in the derivation of these sentences.

The two are not merely notational variants: ideally, the notion of surface structure constraints should make possible the abandonments of conditions on transformational rules. Given a deep structure P_1, a surface structure constraint C on P_n, and a number of transformational rules $T_1 \ldots T_k$, all of them free to apply, there are a number of possible derivations which produce final strings $P_{n1} \ldots P_{n2}k$. The surface structure constraint will then reject all and only those final strings that are incompatible with it.

It is easy to see how such a schema would accommodate the $V/2$ constraint: rather than constraining the transformations themselves (such as fronting, *es*-insertion, and subject-verb inversion, depending on the base from which the derivation proceeds), why not let them simply apply when their structural descriptions are met? The $V/2$ constraint will then reject those sentences in which the finite verb is not the second constituent.

The first problem with this proposal is that it will not predict the ungrammaticality of sentences (7) in Chapter 1, reproduced for convenience below:

(7) (a) *Der Frühling kommt (*es).*
      'Spring is coming.'

  (b) *Ein König lebt (*es) einmal.*

'Once there lived a king.'

(c) *Jeder Mensch hat (*es) seine Schwächen.*

'Everybody has his weaknesses.'

Mechanically, we predict the ungrammaticality of these sentences by an ordering relation between FRONTING and *es*-INSERTION. Given this condition, and the structural description of the latter rule, no problems need arise. But ordering of rules is a condition on their application as much as any other (cf. Lakoff, 1970); if ordering relations are to be permitted, then why not 'if-then conditions' such as those proposed for *VSO* derivations in the last chapter? And if conditions on the application of rules are necessary, then one of the greatest attractions of independent surface structure constraints disappears.

More basically, the problem with a *V*/2 constraint stated as in independent surface structure condition is not that it does not predict the ordering of the rule of *es*-insertion, but rather that it fails to predict even the existence of such a rule. And yet this rule should be predictable.

In the last chapter, we attempted to demonstrate with unequivocal examples that the rule of *es*-insertion, unlike other rules, perhaps, existed in German FOR A REASON: the satisfaction of the *V*/2 constraint. Any theory which fails to recognize the teleology of this rule, as a theory of independent surface structure constraints must fail, does not correctly describe the relevant facts.

We will now attempt to show that a similar situation exists in Spanish, and that a theory of independent surface structure constraints will not explain even some of the facts originally adduced for its justification: the order of pronominal clitics.

Using the fixed order of object pronoun clitics in Spanish as his most telling example, Perlmutter (1971) demonstrated that independent surface structure constraints were needed to perform a filtering function that could be done by neither phrase structural rules or transformational rules, however ordered.

Rather, the acceptable order of clitics had to be represented in the form of a traditional morpheme order chart that was specified independently of the transformational component. Any sequence of clitics that was not a subsequence of the chart

(1)   *se* II I III

was to be rejected if it occurred in surface structure. (In this chart, the Roman numerals stand for person, irrespective of number, gender, or case; only ONE pronoun could go into a given slot, hence it is impossible for two pronouns of the same person to cooccur in the same slot, even if they are correctly ordered with respect to all the other pronouns in the sequence.)

Two cases were described in which well-formed deep structures could never be mapped on to well-formed surface structures by productive grammatical rules:

(i) The surface structure constraint (1) clashes with another surface structure constraint. The satisfaction of the one automatically means the violation of the other.

For example, a large number of middle verbs like *escapar se* 'to escape', may take dative objects. In the case of this verb, the dative object is the person from whom the escape is made. A surface structure constraint specifies that the reflexive clitic must precede the dative clitic (Perlmutter, 1971, 25):

(2)   reflexive dative

Now imagine a sentence like 'I escaped from you', a perfectly grammatical and sensible sentence. In Spanish, however, it is impossible to cliticize the dative object: by (1), the order of clitics must be II I, but by (2), it must be I II. And so, remarkably, no grammatical sentence is possible:

(3) (a)   **Me te escapé.* (violates (1))
    (b)   **Te me escapé.* (violates (2))
          'I escaped from you.'

(ii) The reflexive clitic *se* may have various syntactic origins, all of them independent:

(a) reflexivization with a third person subject
(b) the realization of an underlying structure *PRO* + *VP* (cf. (29) of Chapter 1)
(c) a 'spurious-*se*'-rule.

The last of these rules is shown to be a transformation that converts a dative third person object pronoun to *se* when it precedes another third person pronoun clitic:

(4) (a) *Le recomendé ese hotel.*
'I recommended this hotel to him.'
   (b) **Le lo recomendé.* ⇒
'I recommended it to him.'
   (c) *Se lo recomendé.*
'I recommended it to him.' (by the spurious-*se*-rule)

Often sequences are generated with more than one *se* in surface structure. Since only one clitic can go into each slot, all *se se (se)* sequences are rejected (Perlmutter, 1971, 29-30).

Perlmutter considers three ways of blocking these ungrammatical sequences when they arise:

(a) Constraining optional transformations to prevent them from applying. For example, Spanish, like English, has a rule of sentence pronominalization, whereby an entire sentence can be reduced to a third person singular pronoun: it may then be the second of two third person pronouns in a sequence, whereupon the spurious-*se*-rule would have to apply; but there may also be in the same sequence another *se* pronoun, in which case an ungrammatical **se se* sequence of clitics would arise. Thus sentence pronominalization would have to be blocked only if the subsequent application of the spurious-*se*-rule yielded a violation.

(b) Causing obligatory transformations, such as cliticization, to block. This would have to be done in (3), which could be rendered grammatical only if the dative object were not reduced:

(5)   *Me escapé a te.*
         'I escaped from you.'

(c) Using independent surface structure constraints to reject unacceptable derivations (Perlmutter, 1971, 31-33).

The first and second of these were rejected for two reasons: in the first place, given the theory of grammar at the time, constraints on transformations could be stated only at the point in the derivation at which the transformations themselves applied. But the surface structure constraint would not necessarily be violated until later on in the derivation, when other transformational rules had also applied.

In the second place, the resulting ungrammaticality was a purely superficial fact which would have to be mentioned in the grammar as such in any case, and therefore had nothing to do with the transformations themselves: to constrain the transformations would result in missing a generalization which could be stated for once and for all as a surface structure constraint (Perlmutter, 1971, 35).

It may well be that simply to CONSTRAIN a transformation, as Perlmutter claimed, is completely beside the point. But now let us consider more closely a rule that is crucial to his analysis, the spurious-*se*-rule itself.

As we have seen, this is a transformation that effects the following structural change (following Perlmutter, 1971, 22):

$$
(6) \qquad \begin{bmatrix} \text{III} \\ \text{dative} \end{bmatrix} \begin{bmatrix} \text{III} \\ \text{accusative} \end{bmatrix} \Rightarrow \text{se, 2}
$$
$$
\qquad\qquad\quad 1 \qquad\qquad 2
$$

An irrefutable mass of evidence is presented, conclusively establishing both the existence and the form of this rule. It applies obligatorily whenever its structural description is met. (It is interesting, however, to observe that Perlmutter proposes to abandon conditions of this sort on the application of transformations: "It is no longer necessary for the spurious-*se*-rule to be obligatory, since sentences in which it has failed to apply will be

discarded as ungrammatical by the surface structure constraint."
[1968, chapter 4, fn. 22; cf. Perlmutter, 1971, 128]).

He suggests no reason for the existence of such a rule in the first
place. When we address ourselves to this question, we observe

(a)   that the rule is totally arbitrary. There is absolutely no reason,
      syntactic, semantic, or phonological, why the third person
      object pronouns *le* and *les* should be converted to *se* in surface
      structure. They could with as much justification be converted
      to *lo*, *los*, *la*, or *las*, or indeed, almost anything else.

(b)   that the rule is functionally motivated by the surface structure
      constraint (1): the rule takes as its input a sequence III III
      which is ruled as ungrammatical by the constraint, and converts
      it into *se* III, a sequence which the constraint allows.

Only one motivation for the rule of spurious-*se*-generation is
possible: the peculiar surface structure constraint with which it is
compatible. Both the structural description of this rule and the
structural change that it effects are uniquely determined by (1).

Accordingly, a large number of well-formed deep structures
which would otherwise fail to have acceptable surface realizations,
do in fact have a grammatical shape because of the existence of this
rule.

One can always claim that the spurious-*se*-rule is an accident in
Spanish, with incidental benefits of this nature that are of no
systematic significance in themselves. Languages are replete with
accidents, and the spurious-*se*-rule may well be one of them.

We prefer, however, to adopt the more interesting hypothesis
that the spurious-*se*-rule in Spanish, like the rule of *es*-insertion
in German, is a rule that exists for a reason, namely, the satisfaction
of the language-particular constraints (1) in this chapter 2 and (1)
in chapter 1, respectively. We further make the claim that only
languages which have such constraints on surface structure will
have such rules in their grammars.

As long as we entertain this hypothesis, we cannot be satisfied
by a theory of independent surface structure constraints. Such a

theory, while rejecting unacceptable strings of morphemes, will not specify that languages have a specific mechanism whereby these unacceptable strings are avoided.

In fact, all the classical treatments of output conditions will be deficient in some way.

At least three possible descriptions of output conditions have something of a historical tradition behind them now.

(i) Thesis: Item Arrangement

In a static structuralist description, all constituents would be arranged in a morpheme order chart. From this chart it would be possible to extract the generalization that whatever constituent in a German sentence came first, the verb came second. In Spanish, the order of clitics would be defined in the same way.

(ii) Antithesis: Transformational Derivation

This approach is best exemplified by Bach's proposed treatment of the verb in German. In all sentences, the position of the verb could be predicted by the assumption of a well-motivated deep structure, and the application of productive transformational rules.

The strongest possible claim that can be made within the framework of this approach is that all surface structure configurations follow from the application of independently motivated rules.

(iii) Synthesis: Transformations and Filters

Perlmutter's surface structure constraints, like morpheme order charts, are not the output of generative rules, but unlike morpheme order charts as traditionally conceived, they must screen the output of such rules.

In an item and arrangement description, it would be impossible to recognize the very existence of transformational rules such as that of *es*-insertion in German and spurious-*se*-generation in Spanish.

Within a transformational theory which includes only transformations, it would of course be possible to account for the existence of such rules, and it would have to be possible to account for all surface structure orders by the proper statement and ordering of transformational rules alone. This, however, is precisely what Perlmutter (1971) has demonstrated cannot be done in the case of object clitics in Spanish: that is, there can exist NO transformational rule which could reorder clitics properly. (The argument is basically that such a rule could not be ORDERED with respect to the spurious *se*-rule or be an ANYWHERE RULE, free to apply at any point in the derivation when its structural description was met.)

Perlmutter's approach is the most powerful of the three enumerated here, since it incorporates features of both the other two. In this analysis, the rules of *es*-insertion and spurious *se*-generation would apply optionally when their structural description was met, and the resulting surface structure would be independently assessed by the relevant surface structure condition.

Now, both these rules are certainly statable in generative grammar. In fact, they are very easy to state. Yet they are also very odd rules, which we would not except to find recurring in other languages. Somehow, we must take cognizance of this fact in a theory of grammar.

To do this, let us try, however, imprecisely, to characterize the notion 'natural rule' in syntax.

Arguments of naturalness in phonological theory are by this time familiar; using the theory of markedness and making progressive revisions in the naming of distinctive features, investigators have made efforts to make 'unnatural rules' more expensive and harder to state in a grammar.

For example, Lightner (1968) noted the existence of the Russian *ikan'e*-rule, which could only be stated in traditional features in the following way:

$$(7) \qquad V \to [+\text{high}] \Big/ \begin{bmatrix} C \\ +\text{palatalized} \end{bmatrix} \begin{bmatrix} \underline{\quad\quad} \\ -\text{stress} \end{bmatrix}$$

He argued that the use of separate distinctive features PALATALIZED and HIGH tended to obscure the fact that (7) was an assimilation rule. As stated, the rule could as easily have made the vowel -VOICE after the palatalized consonant, and yet in fact this is not an equally probable result. Therefore, Lightner urged a revision in distinctive feature theory that would reveal (7) as a natural rule: in this case, to mark the relevant feature as the same for vowels and consonants, so that (7) could be stated as an ALPHA rule, whereby the vowel was made to agree in value with the preceding consonant for a feature HIGH.

The explicit claim made within such an amendment is that assimilation rules are natural processes, and that we should probably expect to find them recurring rather frequently.

To the best of my knowledge, no comparable formal revisions have been attempted to define what constitutes a natural rule in syntax. Yet empirically, the situation in syntax is much the same as that in phonology. Certain rules, or types of rules, are found to recur frequently in a variety of languages.

In an early discussion of such rules, Bach (1961) pointed out that the transformations which effect relative clause formation in English, with only minor modifications, would also do the same job in such unrelated languages as Japanese and Swahili. Not unreasonably, he suggested that a componential analysis of many common rules of English would reveal the existence of sub-rules that would be found in most languages. Most of the differences in the surface structures of various languages would then result from different selections and different orders in which these sub-rules would apply, or from certain language-independent universal conditions. For example, Japanese, being a verb-final language, must have relative clauses precede the head noun phrase that they modify in surface structure. This would follow from one of Greenberg's (1963) proposed language universals, which Bach restates as:

$(8) \qquad (S \to NP\ NP\ V) \supset$ (relative clause precedes noun phrase)

In other words, there exists a universal store of syntactic rules shared by different languages. The grammar of individual languages will to a large extent consist of selections from this store.

In his thesis, Ross (1967) also came to grips with the problem of universal rules, and suggested that there could be SKELETON RULES shared by many languages, but fleshed out by them in different ways.

It is then logical to suppose that whatever is language-particular about a given rule should be defined as arbitrary, and belonging to the inventory of those conditions that make the language distinctive; universal grammar, by a process of subtraction, would consist of those rules that are shared by all (or, perhaps, most) languages. The number of skeleton rules shared by these languages is probably quite high.

Consequently, a satisfactory answer to the question: "what is a natural rule?" should involve nothing less than a definition of the limits of universal grammar. This will probably be one of the major concerns of grammatical investigation for some time. But in the meantime, it is probably safe to say that we will find rules like TOPICALIZATION, REFLEXIVIZATION, and IMPERATIVE FORMATION in most languages, and rules like *es*-INSERTION and the SPURIOUS-*se*-RULE in hardly any.

Generally, we may predict that NO language will have a rule of *es*-INSERTION (or anything similar), unless it also has the $V/2$ constraint. NO language will have a rule of SPURIOUS *se*-GENERATION unless it has a surface structure constraint like (1).

Conversely, we can predict the form that such rules will take in the languages in which they do occur. In no language will we find a rule of the form

(9) $\#\,\#\,V \Rightarrow V$ es

if that language has a $V/2$ constraint, and, in general:

(10)   If a sequence which violates a language-particular surface structure constraint is the input to a language-particular rule, then if the rule affects the sequence at all, its output will conform to that constraint.

We thus claim that (17) in chapter 1 and (6) in this chapter are not part of the universal stock of skeleton rules. They will be found only in languages with specific surface structure constraints, and they will always be of such a form as to satisfy these constraints.

Now it is clear that to state only the rule and constraints that are involved would mean to miss the fact that these rules are subordinated to a specific goal; conversely, to state only the goal would mean to miss the fact that the language in question has a mechanism for satisfying the goal, and goes about it in a certain way.

What is needed to describe the verbal position constraint in German is a theory which explicitly relates transformations to the surface structures that they produce and recognizes their interdependence. Such a theory would bear the same relation to a theory of independent surface structure constraints as generative semantics bears to autonomous syntax. The latter, I believe, is justly characterized by the premiss that syntactic transformations and semantic interpretation rules are formally distinct operations. In exactly the same way, it is claimed that surface structure constraints have nothing to do with the application of transformations. The principal consideration which justified their inclusion in grammatical theory was the demonstration that they did work that had to be done, but could not be done by transformational rules.

But when rules are not merely constrained but in fact MOTIVATED by the existence of surface structure constraints, then it is necessary to relate the two rather more intimately than is suggested by Perlmutter's amendment to the standard theory.

Let us now reconsider how ungrammatical sequences of object pronoun clitics may arise in Spanish, and how they may be avoided. As we have already seen, there may be diverse syntactic origins for surface structure *se*. When more than two such sources are present within the same sentence, it does not necessarily follow that the sentence will become ungrammatical: instead an otherwise optional or even an otherwise obligatory rule may be blocked, so that no *se se* output may arise. In his thesis, Perlmutter claimed that it was not only misguided but impossible to put constraints on the relevant transformations, since the derivational history of the sentence is not available at the time that the constraint would have to be operative.

Even within the framework outlined in Perlmutter's analysis, this objection cannot be sustained. Consider the sentence (5), which is compatible with the constraint (1). An otherwise obligatory rule in its derivation - CLITICIZATION of the dative object – has been blocked. WERE IT NOT FOR THE SURFACE STRUCTURE CONSTRAINT (1), the sentence (5) would be marked as ungrammatical for this reason alone. As it stands, however, it is grammatical. At the very least, therefore, a grammar of Spanish must take recognition of the fact that the rule and the constraint are related. A full discussion of the mechanism whereby this could be accomplished would be premature (cf. Lakoff, 1971), but a few general remarks can be made on the subject now.

First, note that it is impossible simply to have the constraint weeding out unacceptable derivations produced by the unconstrained application of the rules. Cliticization must be specified as an obligatory rule to prevent the derivation of countless ungrammatical sentences which could otherwise not be avoided, e.g.:

(11)   *Me escapé a el.
         'I escaped from him.' (non-emphatic reading)

Given this fact, sentences like (5) could not even be derived. The point is that the obligatory requirement on the application of cliticization is relaxed precisely to accommodate the surface structure constraint. So, even for the derivation of (5), it must be possible for the transformation of CLITICIZATION to have access to later information.

This can no longer be considered an unacceptable requirement. Recent work by King (1970), Lakoff (1970), and Andrews (1971) have demonstrated a need for derivational constraints of a global nature, which limit or define the applicability of transformations with reference to different points in the derivations in which these transformations actually apply.

Given the necessity for global rules and derivational constraints, it seems likely that some surface structure constraints must be analyzed as the result of the transformational rules that produce them. This is especially true in the case of constraints such as (1) in chapter 1 in German and (1) in this chapter in Spanish, where otherwise arbitrary and unmotivated rules seem to exist for no other purpose than to satisfy the surface structure constraints of the language in which they appear.

The notion of 'conspiracies' implies a cooperation between surface structure and all the means that a language may utilize to achieve it, whatever they may be.

As such, it is naturally subsumed in a comprehensive theory of derivational constraints, whose central thesis is that all stages of a derivation from semantic representation to surface structure may be relevant, and may have to be available, in determining the form and the applicability of a particular rule.

3

V/2 IN ENGLISH, FRENCH, ROMANSH

With the present exception of English, the *V/2* constraint is shared by all the Germanic languages.

Yet, in the past, English was no more an exception to this constraint than were any other of these languages. In declarative sentences, the finite verb generally came second, whichever constituent came first (Maetzner, 1874, 536; Curme, 1931, 346). It is dangerous to talk of more than TENDENCIES in Old English, where verb-third order was possible 'for rhetorical effect' at all times (Smith, 1893, 221). But the *V/2* tendency is well attested and there are a surprising number of survivals even in modern English.

After sentence-initial demonstrative adverbs, subject-verb inversion in Old English was an almost unshakable rule (Andrew, 1940, 1):

(1) (a) *Þa for Iulius to Rome.*
         'Then went Julius to Rome.'
     (b) *Þonne cymþ se Antecrist.*
         'Then will come the Antichrist.'
     (c) *Þær besæt hie se cyning.*
         'There besieged them the king.'
     (d) *Þa þuhte us eallen þæt Helmstan moste gan forþ.*
         'Then it seemed to all of us that Helmstan should be permitted to go forth.'

The same inversion is found frequently in Elizabethan prose and poetry, and even in modern English:

(2) (a) There goes Max.
     (b) Pop goes the weasel.
     (c) Up jumped the swagman and grabbed him with glee.

But inversion can no longer apply when the subject is a pronoun: Shakespeare could say (in sonnet **XXX**), "Then can I drown an eye", but we can not say:

(3) (a) *There goes he.
    (b) *Pop goes he.
    (c) *Up jumped he.

Inversion was common also after direct quotes, so that if the quotation stood first, the subject followed the verb of saying:

(4) (a) *Hvæt scal ic winnan, cvæð he.*
        "What shall I win?' He said.'
    (b) *Ne wene ic, cwæð Orosius.*
        "I don't know,' said Orosius.'
    (c) *Sigeferð is mîn nama, cvæð he.*
        "Sigeferd is my name,' he said.'

Inversion of this sort has persisted to the present time, but again, is generally confined to non-pronominal subject noun phrases:

(5) (a) 'Harry', said Max, 'leave my daughter alone.'
    (b) 'Harry', he said, 'leave my daughter alone.'

With quotations, subject-verb inversion seems to have become so fixed that it takes place even when these quotes are not fronted, and accounts for not a few cases of verb-initial order in English at all stages of its development:

(6) (a) *Sayde the kynge, 'I geve him leve.'*
    (b) Quoth the raven, 'Nevermore.'

Similarly, inversion accompanied fronting of a predicate adjective or of a predicate noun phrase:

(7) (a) *Sigeferð is mîn nama.*
    (b) *Hælig eart þu.*
        'Holy art thou.'
    (c) So foul lechour was the king.
    (d) High stomached are they both.

In the modern language, it is still possible to prepose predicate noun phrases, particularly proper names, whereupon subject-verb inversion is absolutely necessary:

(8)   Max is my name.

But it is awkward to prepose predicate adjectives under any circumstances. If an adjective is fronted and subject-verb inversion takes place, the result is an affected archaism:

(9)   Very old are the woods.

If no subject-verb inversion takes place, predicate adjective fronting imparts a distinct ethnic flavour to the sentence in which it has applied:

(10)   Beautiful my daughter isn't.

A distinction between full noun phrases and pronouns shows up when the copula verb over which fronting applies is negated. While (9) may sound archaic, (11) is simply impossible:

(11)(a)   *Very old are not the woods.
    (b)   *Very old are the woods not.

But if the subject noun phrase is a pronoun, inversion may still take place and produce an acceptable, if archaic, sentence:

(12)   Very old are they not.

Note that this is exactly the opposite to what previous examples like (3) and (5) may have led us to expect: in those sentences, subject-verb inversion was possible only with non-pronominal noun phrase subjects; in (12), inversion is possible only with pronominal noun phrase subjects.

We will not attempt an explanation of these phenomena here, for two reasons, the first of which carries particular weight: no explanation is known. In any case, our aim is only to demonstrate the *V*/2 tendency in English, and this aim, at least, is well within our reach.

To continue with some further examples: when the direct or

indirect object is preposed, it was usually the case that the verb followed it directly in Old English, a usage which was continued up to Elizabethan English, but not to the present time:

(13) (a) *Þis cvæð se Hæland on his hâlgan godspelle.*
'This said the Saviour in his holy gospel.'

   (b) *Feala vorda gespræc se engel.*
'Many words spoke the angel.'

   (c) Our Lorde Gode wurchip we.

   (d) Full many a deynte hors hadde he in stable.

   (e) Silver and gold have I none.

It is possible that the last of these preposed objects should be more correctly identified as a partitive genitive. These too could be preposed in Old English, whereupon subject-verb inversion had to follow:

(14) (a) *And þyses wæs Ælfgar to gewitnesse.*
'And of this was Ælfgar as witness.'

   (b) *And þissera gewritu syndan þreo.*
'And there are three of these writs.'

Moreover, subject-verb inversion was fairly regular when any adverb was fronted, and continues to be just barely acceptable in some archaic forms of English today, whether the adverb is a single word or phrase, or a dependent subordinate clause of time, manner, place, or circumstance:

(15) (a) *Gif hit þonne festendæg sie, selle mon weæge cæse.*
'If it is then a feastday, one may give a wey of cheese.'

   (b) *Þa we hie æt Weardoran nu semdan, þa bær mon þa boc forþ.*
'When we now brought them to agreement at Wardour, one of them brought the deed forth.'

   (c) Not as the world giveth give I unto you.

   (d) Yet have I left a daughter.

   (e) Three times were the Romans driven back.

   (f) So ended his tale.

The only inheritance that survives from this usage is subject-verb inversion after the adverbs *only, scarcely, hardly, under no conditions,* and others of that class, characterized by Klima (1964) as AFFECTIVE.

(16)(a) Never had there been such an uproar.
  (b) Not until the train had left did I realize that someone had stolen my wallet.
  (c) Under no conditions will I ever forgive her.

Inversion after these adverbs always occurred (Maetzner, 1874, 541) but the interesting fact is that it took place after all sentence-initial adverbs equally. This is no longer the case in English, which suggests that one possible type of syntactic change is the semantic specialization of a once general rule.

As we know, English now differs from German in allowing the finite verb to occur as the third constituent in declarative sentences, and this is the chief point of variance between the two languages as regards word order. A full discussion of how this change may have occurred follows in the next part; for the present, however, we need only note that the change occurred comparatively recently, and that at one time English conformed to the Germanic type in complying with the *V*/2 constraint.

Nor are the Germanic languages alone in observing the constraint. In the eleventh and twelfth centuries it was also shared by French, and constituted "une des règles les mieux établies de la syntaxe médiévale" (Dauzat, 1930, 436-437). This phenomenon has been extensively discussed in a large number of syntactic analyses of the poetry and prose of the period, notably Morf, 1878, Schlickum, 1882, Ebering, 1881, and Thurneysen, 1892, from which most of the following examples are culled:

(17)(a) *Mais en enfer voil jou aler.*
    'But to hell wish I to go.'
  (b) *Encor ai je ci une bone espee.*
    'Yet have I here a good sword.'
  (c) *Bele douce ami, fait il.*
    '"Beautiful sweet friend", said he.'

(d) *Tant n'atendroie je mie.*
'So much would I never expect.'

(e) *Les dis mulez fait Carles establer.*
'The ten mules Charles has taken to the stable.'

(f) *Mess e matines ad li reis escultet.*
'Mass and Matins has the king heard.'

In modern French as in modern English, fronting of a constituent other than the subject does not usually cause subject-verb inversion to apply, except for a small number of adverbs, among them *encore*, 'yet', *aussi* 'therefore' and some others which still require inversion.

The currently spoken Romansh dialects of Switzerland also obey the $V/2$ constraint exactly as do the neighbouring dialects of German. A few examples from the Vallader dialect will serve to illustrate this point:

(18)(a) *Eir per quai savain- a grà.*
'Also for this are-we grateful.'

(b) *Da la versiun existan 3 dactiloscrits.*
'Of the rendering there exist three typed copies.'

(c) *Iminchacas reprodüa Lansel eir in rumantsch la mezzarima.*
'In any case, Lansel also reproduces the half-rhyme in Romansh.'

The situation is thus exactly the same as in German and in medieval French.

So far, we have investigated only one aspect of the means whereby these languages obey the $V/2$ constraint, namely how they avoid verb-third position by putting the subject after the verb when some other constituent has been fronted. German, as we have seen, also avoids verb-initial position by means of a transformation of *es*-INSERTION. All the other Germanic languages and French and Romansh have analogues to this transformation, and the syntactic investigation of the differences between them is the dominant theme of the following part.

The origins of the $V/2$ constraint in Germanic may remain a subject of dispute: we conjecture, on the basis of some of the oldest texts, that the proto-language inherited superficial verb-final order (Paul, 1919, 75; Maurer, 1926, 184) and that the successor languages, among them Old High German, rapidly abandoned it in favour of verb-initial and verb-second order.

But we may certainly attempt to explain the *V*/2 constraint in the Romance dialects of French and Romansh by reference to Germanic influence alone.

Various authors have maintained that French could have inherited the *V*/2 constraint directly from Latin. Thurneysen (1892, 300), noting that Latin was already beginning to shift the finite forms of the verbs *esse* 'to be' and *habere* 'to have' into second position, contended that French may have simply generalized this tendency. Lerch (1934, 381) pointed out that the Latin of the Vulgate Bible did indeed have verb-second order for other verbs besides these two:

(19)   *In principio creavit Deus caelum et terram.*
         'In the beginning created God Heaven and earth.'

Moreover, verb-second order was found occasionally in Old Spanish and Italian as well.

Yet that the *V*/2 constraint was simply inherited from Latin seems to me an implausible contention for two reasons.

In the first place, the earliest French monuments that we possess, dating from the eighth century, are written in a language which has much in common with the Latin from which it descended, in particular, verb-final order in declarative sentences (Brunot, 1905, 264). It is only in the *Chanson de Roland*, written perhaps four hundred years later (Bédier, 1924), that we find verb-second order, and find it consistently.

In the second place, even if a tendency to move the main verb into second position was inherited from Latin, the fact would remain that Latin, like Spanish and Italian, was never more than half-hearted in satisfying this tendency, while in French there were scarcely any exceptions to the *V*/2 constraint.

Given the depth and the intensity of German influence on French, and the lack of any such influence on Spanish and Italian, we are surely justified in suggesting that German at least reenforced whatever tendency French may have had in the first place to satisfy the $V/2$ constraint.

Brunot, the most eminent historian of the French language, cautiously refrains from attributing any syntactic changes to French influence, and comments frequently on the paucity of syntactic data in general. But when speaking of lexical borrowing between the two languages in the crucial period between the eighth and twelfth centuries, he can confidently assert that "il n'y a donc pas des emprunts du roman au germanique, mais, dans une certaine sens, UNE VÉRITABLE INTERPÉNÉTRATION DE L'UN PAR L'AUTRE... il importe toutefois de retenir qu'elle a été plus forte qu'aucune autre." (Brunot, 1905, 129; small capitals added).

As for the Swiss dialects of Romansh, the depth and the extent of Swiss German influence upon them is a matter of bitter record. (For two recent discussions, cf. Weinreich, 1953; Cavigelli, 1969.)

These, then, are the languages that share the $V/2$ constraint, either now or at some time in their history: the Germanic languages; French; and the Romansh dialects of Switzerland.

PART II

A HISTORICAL SURVEY

4

THE TYPE A CONSTRAINT

In the final chapter of his study, "Deep and Surface Structure Constraints in Syntax", Perlmutter (1971) suggested the following typological distinction among the world's languages: either they must, like French, provide all verbs inflected for tense with subjects in surface structure, or, like Spanish, they may dispense with superficial subjects. Languages of the former variety, among them French, and English, were labelled type A languages, while those of the latter sort were classified as type B. Noting that Latin was a type B language, but that French was a type A language, Perlmutter suggested that the change from type B to type A was a possible historical change, but he suggested no reason for the existence of this change in such a language as French, and its absence in Spanish.

We are now able to propose a possible motivation for the type A surface structure constraint in the languages where it obtains. But first a brief review of the status of the type A: type B distinction will be useful.

Perlmutter's blanket classification was useful because it related a number of seemingly disparate phenomena in French and Spanish, and other languages as well. Although these phenomena must indeed be related, it is my belief that Perlmutter's account of the unifying constraint is not entirely accurate, in that it makes predictions that are at times too weak, and at other times too strong.

In the first case, the type A constraint as it is stated is not always a mere surface structure constraint, but applies at earlier stages of the derivation: in this sense the constraint is too weak. In the second case, there are instances where a surface structure subject is not required in type A languages for grammatical sentences: in this sense the constraint is too strong.

I will first recapitulate the allegedly related phenomena, adding one that seems to have been overlooked, and then show that some of them, at least, are independent of the constraint as it is presently defined.

(i) Constraints on movement rules

Consider the following two sentences:

(1) (a)　Who did you say that you saw?
　　　(b)　*Who did you say that saw you?

It is claimed that type A languages, like English, do not allow movement transformations to remove subject pronouns from clauses with finite verbs, although the same movement rules are free to move non-subject noun phrases. Therefore (1a) is grammatical and (1b) is not.

If the subject noun phrase is removed by SUBJECT RAISING, no violation results, because the subordinate clause from which raising takes place no longer has a finite verb:

(2) (a)　I was expecting Max to arrive.
　　　(b)　Who were you expecting to arrive?

Perlmutter claimed that languages like Spanish and Italian allow such movement rules as take place in (1b), since, unlike French and English, they do not have a constraint on the presence of subjects for tense-inflected verbs in surface structure within the same clause. Thus, the Italian sentences which follow are grammatical:

(3) (a)　*Chi hai detto che è a casa?*
　　　　　'Who did you say that was at home?'
　　　(b)　*Chi crede Berardo che la sposerebbe?*
　　　　　'Who does Berardo believe that would marry her?
　　　(c)　*Chi hai predetto che sara cornuto?*
　　　　　'Who did you predict that will be a cuckold?'

Whether this fact indeed has anything at all to do with a surface structure constraint of the sort proposed is so questionable that it may be better to leave it out of the discussion entirely. Consider first the perfect grammaticality of the English sentences:

(4) (a) Who did you say saw you?
    (b) The man who I said looked like Boris was his uncle.

The only structural difference between these sentences and the ungrammatical (1b) lies in the deletion in the former of the complementizer *that*. Perlmutter (1968) originally accounted for this difference by claiming that the presence of this complementizer caused the sentence node which dominated it to branch:

When the complementizer is deleted, by a rule that applies optionally in English under certain conditions, the sentence node dominating the subjectless verb phrase no longer branches:

Thereupon, an independently motivated convention of TREE PRUNING (proposed by Ross 1969a; Ross 1967) applies, and the non-branching sentence node is wiped out. Since there is now no sentence left in surface structure, the constraint which rejects subjectless sentences does not apply, and (4a) and (4b) are both grammatical.

This argument is only as strong as the claim that there is one single node *VP*. If it can be shown that instead of a single node *VP*, the predicate phrase of a sentence must consist of several nodes, then tree pruning cannot apply, and the branching argument collapses.

The traditionally accepted argument for the identification of *VP* as a single node was given in an important paper by Lakoff and

Ross (1966), and is based on the so-called *do so*-transformation, which relates the following sentences:

(5) (a) Max gave Mary a book and Sam gave Mary a book. ⇒
    (b) Max gave Mary a book, and Sam did so too.

Using the *do so*-transformation as a criterion for *VP* constituency, Lakoff and Ross demonstrated that a number of adverbial elements that had been traditionally associated with the verb phrase (cf. Chomsky, 1965, 102) such as manner, place and time adverbs, were not in fact to be so associated:

(6) (a) Max accepted defeat glumly, but Sam did so with defiance.
    (b) Max robbed a bank yesterday, and Sam will do so to-morrow.
    (c) Max must kiss his auntie, now that Ingrid has already done so.

The consequences of accepting this criterion for *VP* constituency are twofold: not only are most adverbials to be excluded from the *VP*, but so too are tense (6b) and the so-called auxiliary verbs (6c).

It follows that the predicate phrases of (6) are not exhaustively dominated by the node *VP*, and that for this reason, the *S* node which dominates the *VP* of these sentences branches even when the subject has been removed by some transformation. We would therefore predict that the removal of the complementizer *that* would not save these sentences from ungrammaticality once the subject noun phrase had been moved, as it is in (4). Yet this is not the case:

(7) (a) Who did you say saw you yesterday?
    (b) The man who I said looked like Boris yesterday had again altered his appearance.

It may be argued that the entire predicate phrase, including the verb phrase, is itself dominated by a single node PREDICATE. Indeed the *do so*-transformation itself offers some support for this contention, for this pro-verbal form can replace not only *VP*, which may be defined as the MINIMUM sphere of its applicability, but successively larger phrases up to and including the entire predicate phrase itself:

(8) (a) Max accepted defeat glumly, and Sam did so too.

(b) Max carved the turkey with a pocketknife by accident, and Sam did so with a carbing knife after careful deliberation.

(c) Max carved the turkey with a pocketknife by accident, but Sam did so after careful deliberation.

(d) Max carved the turkey with a pocketknife by accident, and Sam did so too.

That is, the *do so*-transformation, if it applies to single nodes, must apply to a derived structure of the following kind:

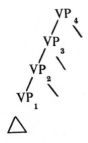

If this is so, sentences like (7) do not constitute evidence against Perlmutter's branching hypothesis, since in each of these cases, the topmost *S* node does not itself branch.

But by the *do so*-criterion, auxiliary verbs like *can* and *must* do not belong to the *VP*, since they can never be replaced by *do so:*

(9) Max must kiss his auntie if Roger does so.

cannot mean

(10) Max must kiss his auntie if Roger must kiss his auntie.

Still going by the *do so*-criterion, we must propose a derived constituent structure of the following sort for (9):

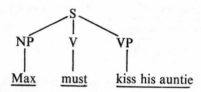

And we therefore predict that the presence of an auxiliary verb in a subjectless sentence will cause that sentence to dominate two nodes, *V* and *VP*, (or *Aux* and *VP*; for a catalogue of arguments for auxiliaries as main verbs, see Ross, 1969b). Consequently, we would predict that the counterparts of (4) with auxiliary verbs would be ungrammatical. Yet this is not so:

(11)(a)　Who did you say could throw a tiger?

　　(b)　Who did you say must have been responsible?

Finally, one could claim, as does Chomsky (1965, 102) that ALL the elements of the predicate phrase, including the auxiliary, were dominated by one node. But such a claim would be unjustified: nodes are demonstrated to exist in a linguistic description, if they are subject to well defined grammatical rules. Thus, the justification of the node NOUN PHRASE included the demonstration that a number of transformations, including the PASSIVE, CLEFTING, and PRO-NOMINALIZATION rules had to refer to such a node. No similar justification exists for any putative node PREDICATE.

In a significant revision of his 1968 thesis, Perlmutter (1971, 112) proposed that S pruning apply, independently of Ross' condition, when the indicative complementizer *that* is deleted.

Such a solution is totally *ad hoc*. More seriously, it fails to account for all the relevant phenomena even in English.

There are a number of interesting facts about subject movement rules in English, which are not even touched on in the foregoing discussion. For example, while it is true that subject noun phrases can be moved out of object complements when the *that*-complementizer has been deleted, no such movement of subject noun phrases from extraposed subject complements is possible:

(12)(a)   It is likely (that) Max will forget the beer.
   (b)   *Who is it likely (that) will forget the beer?
(13)(a)   It seems (that) Max wouldn't bother wearing gloves.
   (b)   *Who does it seem (that) wouldn't bother wearing gloves?

Again, the movement constraint applies only to SUBJECT noun phrases and is not a general constraint on movement out of extraposed clauses:

(14)(a)   What is it likely (that) Max will forget to bring?
   (b)   What does it seem (that) Max wouldn't bother wearing?

To the best of my knowledge, no general principle or constraint has ever been put forward to explain this rather mysterious fact. Nor is it my intention to propose one here. We need not emphasize, however, that sentences like (12) and (13) are also counterevidence to Perlmutter's hypothesis about the interrelation between branching, subject movement, and tree pruning.

Further disconfirming evidence is provided by a number of type B languages which, like Spanish and Italian, should allow subject movement out of subordinate clauses, but fail to do so.

In Serbo-Croatian, Hungarian, and Russian (all of which are true type B languages by the criteria which we accept) subject movement out of lower clauses is no more permitted than it is in English.

(i) Movement rules in Serbo-Croatian

Consider the following sentences:

(15)(a)   *Milan   je   prorekao   da*
          Milan   (aux. 3 sg.)   predicted (3 sg.)   that
                 će   se   njegova   sestra
          (aux. 3 sg. fut.)   (reflexive 3 sg.)   his (fem.)   sister
          venčati   sa   Bogdanom.
          marry   with   Bogdan (instrumental)

'Milan predicted that his sister would marry Bogdan.'

(b) *Ko je Milan prorekao da će se venčati sa Bogdanom?*
'Who did Milan predict that would marry Bogdan?'

(c) *Za koga je Milan prorekao da će se venčati sa Bogdanom?*
'Of whom did Milan say that (she) would marry Bogdan?'

(16)(a) | Misliš | da | nije | kod |
|---|---|---|---|
| think (2 sg. pres.) | that | (neg. +be 3 sg. pres.) | at |

kuće.

home (gen.)

'You think that he isn't at home.'

(b) *Ko misliš da nije kod kuće?*
'Who (nom.) do you think that isn't at home?'

(c) *Za koga misliš da nije kod kuće?*
'Of whom (acc.) do you think that (he) isn't at home?'

Sentences (15b) and (16b) demonstrate that there is a constraint on moving subject noun phrases out of a lower sentence; (15c) and (16c) demonstrate that this constraint has absolutely nothing to do with the putative surface structure constraint: the SURFACE STRUCTURE of the corresponding (b) and (c) subordinate clauses is identical, morpheme for morpheme. In particular, both lack a superficial subject. But in the (b) sentences, the subject was removed by a movement rule, while in the (c) sentences, it was removed by a pronoun deletion rule that applies in, and distinguishes, type B languages in general (discussion of this feature follows).

The constraint, then, is not on surface structure, but on the application of a particular movement rule. Yet movement rules are free to move noun phrases other than the subject, illustrating that the constraint is not a general property of subordinate clauses:

(17)(a) | Ti | si | hteo | da |
|---|---|---|---|
| you (sg.) | (aux. 2 sg.) | wanted (masc. sg.) | that |
| ga | vidiš. | | |
| him (acc.) | see (2 sg.) | | |

'You wanted to see him.'

(b) *Koga si hteo da vidiš?*
'Whom (acc.) did you want to see?'

(18)(a)   *Ti*   *si*   *rekao*   *da*
         you (sg.)   (aux. 2 sg.)   said (masc. sg.)   that
           si   *mu*   *ga*   *dao.*
         (aux. 2 sg.)   him (dat.)   it (acc.)   gave (masc. sg.)
         'You said that you had given it to him.'

    (b)   *Komu si rekao da si ga dao?*
         'To whom (dat.) did you say that you had given it?'

(ii) Movement rules in Hungarian

(19)(a)   *Ferenc*   *már*   *mondta*   *hogy*   *a*   *hug-*
         Frank   already   said (3 sg. def.)   that   the   sister
             a   *Pál-*   *hoz*   *megy*   *férj-*   *hez*
         (3 sg. poss.)   Paul   to   goes   husband   to
         'Frank already said that his (younger) sister would marry
         Paul.'

    (b)   **Ki mondta Ferenc hogy Pálhoz megy férjhez?*
         'Who did Frank say that would marry Paul?'

    (c)   *Kiröl mondta Ferenc hogy Pálhoz megy férjhez?*
         'Of whom did Frank say that (she) would marry Paul?'

(20)(a)   *Mondtad*   *hogy*   *nincs*   *otthon.*
         said (2 sg. def.)   that   (neg. 3 sg. existential)   at home
         'You said that he wasn't at home.'

    (b)   **Ki mondtad hogy nincs otthon?*
         'Who did you say was not at home?'

    (c)   *Kiröl mondtad hogy nincs otthon?*
         'Of whom did you say that (he) was not at home?'

As with the Serbo-Croatian, a comparison of the (b) and (c)
examples will reveal that whatever the constraint on grammaticality
may be, it has nothing to do with the surface structure of the clause
from which subject-movement was supposed to occur. In each of
(b) and (c), the surface structure of the subordinate clause is totally
identical: the ungrammaticality of (b) arises from the fact that a
movement rule, rather than a deletion rule, has taken place, and

this movement rule is blocked in Hungarian, as it is in English and Serbo-Croatian.

As in Serbo-Croatian and English, the movement constraint does apply only to subject noun phrases. Although it is not possible to raise OBJECT noun phrases into higher sentences with transitive matrix verbs (for an entirely different reason, discussed in a recent unpublished paper by Szamosi, 1970), all other non-subject noun phrases can be wrenched out of subordinate clauses without impairing the grammaticality of the resulting sentence:

(21) (a) *Mondtad   hogy   félsz   a   kutyátol.*
        said (2 sg. def.)   that   afraid (2 sg.)   the   dog (abl.)
        'You said that you were afraid of the dog.'

   (b) *Mitöl mondtad hogy félsz?*
        'Of what (abl.) did you say that you were afraid?'

(22) (a) *Mondtad   hogy   egy   kis   macskával*
        said (2 sg. def.)   that   one   little   cat-with
        játszottal.
        played (2 sg. ind.)
        'You said that you had played with a little cat.'

   (b) *Mivel mondtad hogy játszottal?*
        'What (comitative) did you say that you had played with?'

But although the constraint does apply to subject noun phrases only, there can be no question that the constraint is not one on surface structure. Hungarian can offer us a particularly convincing demonstration of this, in that it is possible to construct a potentially 'ambiguous' sentence, with two possible readings, depending on whether the interrogative pronoun *ki* 'who' is the subject of the higher sentence, or of the lower sentence from which it removed by the interrogative movement transformation:

(23)   *Ki   mondta   hogy   nincs*
        who   said (3 sg. def.)   that   (neg. 3 sg. existential)
        otthon?
        at home

Since Hungarian, like other type B languages, allows the deletion of unstressed personal pronoun subjects, it is clear that two readings are possible for (23):

(23) (a) Who$_i$ said that he$_i$ was not at home?

   (b) Who$_i$ did he$_j$ say that was not at home?

In (23a), the subordinate clause *nincs otthon* is subjectless by virtue of the pronoun subject deletion rule which applies in type B languages; in (23b), the subordinate clause has lost its subject by the interrogative transformation which shifts question words to the beginning of the sentence, as in English.

In Hungarian, however, only one reading of (23) is grammatical, and that is the first. The second, with equivalent surface structure, is not. The meaning of (23b) can only be rendered by a sentence in which movement out of the subordinate clause has NOT occurred:

(24)   *Kiröl mondta hogy nincs otthon?*
      'Of whom$_i$ did he$_j$ say that (he$_i$) was not at home?'

Further examples of this type of constraint are surely superfluous. We may note that Russian, another type B language, does not tend to allow movement out of subordinate clauses at all. Yet informants agree that there is a perceptible deterioration of grammaticality when the constituent which has been removed is a subject noun phrase. That the constraint is one on movement rather than on acceptable surface structures can be demonstrated by sentences parallel to the ones that we have used for Serbo-Croatian and Hungarian.

Why languages like Spanish and Italian allow movement rules to remove subjects from lower clauses is a mystery; no less a mystery is why other languages like Hungarian do not, by which I mean simply that to the best of our knowledge at the time, the applicability of the movement constraint is not systematically correlated with any other facts in the grammar of these languages.

Equally mysterious, I would suggest, is why the presence of the complementizer *that* would affect the constraint in English; and why the deletion of the complementizer is allowed to take place in some contexts but not in others.

But it is evident, in my opinion, that surface structure considerations have little to do with the movement constraint, and I accordingly propose that this distinction among languages should be omitted from the inventory of facts for which the type A: type B distinction should be expected to furnish an explanation.

We accordingly turn to some of the other valid distinctions that do seem to correlate with the typological classification that Perlmutter suggested.

(ii) The deletability of personal pronoun subjects

Whereas type A languages do not allow the deletion of personal pronoun subjects, even if no ambiguity would result, type B languages do, even if ambiguity sometimes results from such deletion.

The traditional explanation for deletion, found most frequently in pedagogical grammars of Latin, Italian, Spanish, and other type B languages, written for speakers of English, is that the verbal endings are sufficiently differentiated for the pronoun to be dispensed with. This explanation is at the very least inadequate, since it would predict that a language like Romansh, which has a system of verbal desinences every bit as rich as that of Italian, would, like this language, allow deletion of the unstressed subject pronoun. Yet Romansh, a type A language, does not allow deletion.

Conversely, type B languages allow deletion of subject pronouns even when ambiguity arises as a result.

(iii) Subjects for impersonal verbs

In type A languages, the so-called WEATHER VERBS, which denote natural phenomena, must always occur with surface structure subjects, while among the type B languages, no such subject is necessary. Thus, Latin says *pluit*, while French says *il pleut*, for *it is raining*.

The category of impersonal verbs is a large one, in which we include, at least for now, not only those verbs which denote natural phenomena, but also the transformationally derived impersonal passives and reflexives which describe activities without reference to any particular agent. Like weather verbs, these impersonal verbs are provided with impersonal subjects by type A languages, but not by type B languages. Accordingly, as we have seen, Latin has *pugnatur* 'there is fighting', while German has *es wird gestritten*.

(iv) Indefinite Pronoun Subjects

In type A languages, the subject *PRO* must be spelled out in surface structure as a pronoun. Thus, German *man*, French *on*, and English *we, you, they*, and *one*. In type B languages, such a pronoun, if it exists, is deleted in surface structure. In Russian, as we have seen (p. 27) there must be a distinct *PRO* noun phrase, but unlike *man* and *on*, this is never spelled out in surface structure.

(v) Dummy subjects replace extraposed sentences

The transformation of extraposition relates sentences like those of the following pair:

(25) (a)   That Harry is a leper does not distress me. ⇒
  (b)   It does not distress me that Harry is a leper.

In all type A languages, when extraposition moves a sentential subject away from subject position, a dummy pronoun (e.g. English *it*; German *es*; French *il*) must remain in this position. In type B languages, no such pronoun must appear.

(vi) There-insertion

There-insertion, or German *es*-insertion, is the transformation that relates such sentences as the following:

(26) (a) *A muskrat is in my closet. ⇒
(b) There is a muskrat in my closet.

All type A languages must have a rule of *there*-insertion, or some analogue thereto, when the logical subject of the sentence has been moved away from subject position, and, indeed, is no longer in the syntactic relation SUBJECT-OF, to the sentence in which it appears.

No such rule is found in type B languages.

Now, let us examine these phenomena in some more detail, and attempt to evaluate the correctness of the constraint.

Perlmutter proposes that type A languages are defined by a constraint that states:

(27)   "Any sentence other than an imperative in which there is an *S* that does not contain a subject in surface structure is ungrammatical." (Perlmutter, 1971, 100).

Only this and nothing more.

In at least one case, the constraint as it is stated makes exactly the right predictions about the appearance of pronouns. It is worth considering this case in detail in order to highlight the content of (27).

The indefinite subject pronoun *PRO* does seem to be required only as a subject in those type A languages where it has a particular realization. French *on* and German *man* can occur only in the nominative case, which is exactly what we would expect, given that they only exist in order to satisfy (27). For oblique cases, German uses the appropriate form of *einer* 'one', which, like English *one* does not mean exactly the same thing as *PRO*; while French dispenses with a pronoun entirely:

(28) (a) *Das kann einen böse machen.*
(b) *Cela peut enrager* ———.
'That can make one angry.'

Even when they originate as subject pronouns, these disappear when they have undergone the transformation of SUBJECT RAISING (illustrated in (2a)) a rule that relates sentences like the following pair:

(29) (a)   I was expecting [Max will arrive]$_S$. $\Rightarrow$
   (b)   I was expecting Max to arrive.

Again, this is what we expect: since the noun phrase has been raised out of a clause that no longer has as its main verb a verb inflected for tense, this clause, by (27), does not require the appearance of a superficial realization of *PRO*.

(30) (a)   *Ma femme laisse* [*je sors les poubelles*]$_S$.
   (b)   *Ma femme laisse* [*PRO sort les poubelles*]$_S$.

Once these sentences have undergone subject-raising, the resulting surface structures are:

(31) (a)   *Ma femme me laisse sortir les poubelles.*
       'My wife has me take out the garbage.'
   (b)   *Ma femme laisse* ——— *sortir les poubelles.*
       'My wife has the garbage taken out.'

The same correspondence is to be observed in German:

(32) (a)   *Ich liess* [*er schneidet mir die Haare*]$_S$.
   (b)   *Ich liess* [*PRO schneidet mir die Haare*]$_S$.

When subject raising takes place, the result is:

(33) (a)   *Ich liess ihn mir die Haare schneiden.*
       'I had him cut my hair.'
   (b)   *Ich liess mir die Haare schneiden.*
       'I had my hair cut.'

Even in English, for that matter, similar correspondences are to be observed.

   The English pronouns *they*, *you*, *one*, and *we*, when they serve as indefinite pronouns, can never appear in the agent phrase of a passive sentence:

(34)   Max was robbed * $\left(\text{by} \begin{cases} \text{them} \\ \text{one} \\ \text{you} \\ \text{us} \end{cases} \right)$.

For this reason, indefinite agent deletion applies in the English translations of (31b) and (33b).

Frequently, too, the indefinite pronoun cannot appear as the OBJECT of a transitive verb or adjective:

(35)(a)   This book shocks $\begin{cases} \text{Max} \\ \text{one.} \end{cases}$

   (b)   This book is shocking to $\begin{cases} \text{Max} \\ \text{*one.} \end{cases}$

When in construction with infinitival complements, the English indefinite pronouns also disappear, optionally in some cases, and obligatorily in others. There are two infinitival complementizers in English, the *for-to* and the *poss.-ing* (Rosenbaum, 1967) found in the following two sentences:

(36)(a)   For John to shave himself takes forever.
   (b)   Fred's coming upset our plans.

But now consider sentences with these complementizers, in which the subject of the lower sentence is *PRO:*

(37)(a)   [one shaves oneself]$_S$ takes time.
   (b)   [you shave yourself]$_S$ takes time.

With *for-to* complementizer:

(38)(a)   (for one) to shave onself takes time.
   (b)   (*for you) to shave yourself takes time.

With the *poss. -ing* complementizer:

(39)(a)   (*one's) shaving takes time.
   (b)   (*your) shaving takes time.

Once again, these facts are not surprising, given the correctness of the constraint (27), which specifies the need for these pronouns only as the subjects of verbs inflected for tense.

If constraint (27) were absolutely correct, we would expect to find similar results in each of the cases where the constraint calls for subject pronouns.

But the constraint is too weak in predicting the appearance of such an introductory pronoun as *there* in English. The transformation of *there*-INSERTION is an early rule (for some discussion, cf. McCawley, 1970) in the derivation of English sentences. Subsequent transformations, among them SUBJECT RAISING and COMPLEMENTIZER PLACEMENT may take this pronoun and remove it from the clause in which it originated, leaving behind them infinitival clauses. Constraint (27) would predict that once this had occurred, there would be no need for the dummy subject (NOW OBJECT) *there*, and that, like the English realizations of *PRO*, it could be deleted. This is not so:

(40) (a) I expect [there will be an explosion]$_S$. (raising) ⇒
   (b) I expect there to be an explosion.
   (c) *I expect to be an explosion.
(41) (a) [there will be an explosion]$_S$ would not surprise me. (C.P.) ⇒
   (b) For there to be an explosion would not surprise me.
   (c) *(for) to be an explosion would not surprise me.

In the same way, WEATHER VERBS like 'rain' must be provided with the dummy subject 'it' at an early stage in the derivation of English sentences. Like *there*, this subject must be available for RAISING and COMPLEMENTIZER PLACEMENT, and, like *there*, it cannot be deleted:

(42) (a) Zeus caused [it rains]$_S$. (raising) ⇒
   (b) Zeus caused it to rain.
   (c) *Zeus caused to rain.
(43) (a) [it rains]$_S$ would be disastrous. (C.P.) ⇒
   (b) For it to rain now would be disastrous.
   (c) *(for) to rain now would be disastrous.

Thus the ungrammaticality of the sentences (40c), (41c), (42c), and (43c) indicates that the constraint (27) is TOO WEAK.

Two constructions in which dummy subjects are required in type A languages are impersonal passives, and the so-called *there*-sentences. As we have seen, a constraint that calls for superficial structure subjects only is too weak to account for the latter in English. The transformation analogous to English *there*-insertion is German *es*-insertion, which differs from its English counterpart in several important respects.

As we have demonstrated in chapter one, *es*-insertion both in existential sentences and in impersonal passives need take place only in order to keep the verb in second place in conformity with the word order constraint (1) in chapter 1. It is by no means true that *es* must appear in all clauses with finite verbs, and hence, for these cases at least, the constraint (27) is TOO STRONG.

These facts taken together would suggest that the constraint (27) is almost unsalvageable. Yet Perlmutter's insight that all the phenomena which are shared by type A languages must be related by some generalization, should not, I think, be abandoned. It is only the nature of this generalization which is in question.

Among those type A languages mentioned in Perlmutter's study were English, French, and German. To these we may add the remaining Germanic languages and Romansh. The type B languages which he enumerated included Latin, Spanish, and Italian, Arabic, Walbiri, Hebrew, Hausa, and Basque. To these we may add the remaining Romance languages, all the Slavic languages, and all the other Indo-European languages attested at any time, as well as the Uralic languages, the Altaic languages, and, apparently, most of the other languages of the world.

As it was originally presented, the typological distinction which Perlmutter proposed was unintentionally misleading, in that it suggested that languages could belong to one or the other group independently of genetic affiliation. The most unambiguous evidence in support of this was the behaviour of French, which was and is a type A language, while both Latin, its ancestor, and Spanish, its sister dialect, are not.

However, it seems to me that when a larger number of languages are considered, the genetic independence of type A structure is more apparent than real. With the exception of French and Romansh, the class of type A languages is coextensive with the Germanic languages.

As we have established in chapter three, a structural feature that is shared by the Germanic languages, French, and Romansh, is that they are all, or have all at one time been, languages with the $V/2$ constraint: the former group probably by heredity, and the latter two probably by borrowing from Germanic dialects.

This coincidence encourages us to formulate the hypothesis that:

(44)   Only those languages which have or have had the $V/2$ constraint can ever be type A languages.

In the following chapters, I would like to examine a few type A languages, and show that the presence of pronominal subjects in each of them was once more obviously dependent on the $V/2$ target in all of them than it now is; indicate stages of the process whereby the presence of superficial subjects became independent of this constraint in general; venture on a description of these stages; and finally propose a possible mechanism of syntactic change, which would account for the changes that we may observe.

Before continuing, we resume our definition of type A languages, which must exhibit ALL of the following characteristics:

(i)   Allow no deletion of unstressed personal pronoun subjects.
(ii) Must have subjects for impersonal verbs.
(iii) Have special indefinite pronoun subjects like *on* and *man*.
(iv) Have dummy subjects to replace extraposed sentences.
(v)   Have a dummy pronoun *there* (or some equivalent) to stand in the place of logical subjects that have been displaced from sentence-initial position.

We do not specify the conditions under which these requirements may be relaxed in the various type A languages, and as we shall see, these conditions differ from one language to another, and even from one historical stage to another of the same language.

5

GOTHIC AND ICELANDIC

By our criterion of what constitutes a type A language, two Germanic languages fail to qualify for this status. Significantly, neither seems to have had the *V*/2 constraint.

In Gothic, a language which survives today largely through Wulfila's translation of the Bible, word order in general seems to have been characterized by a slavish devotion to the Greek original from which the Bible was translated (Streitberg, 1906, 181). Although word order in spoken Gothic undoubtedly differed in many crucial respects from that of Greek, it hardly seems likely that Wulfila would have consistently violated a rigorous word order constraint in his own language in order to adhere to the original in a work that was intended for more or less popular consumption.

Personal pronoun subjects were usually omitted, except under special contrastive stress (Streitberg, 1906, 175). The only impersonal verb attested in the corpus, 'to rain', occurs without a superficial subject:

(1) (a) *Jah rigneith ana garaihtans.*
and rains on righteous
'For it rains on the righteous...'
(b) *Rignida swibla ja funin.*
rained sulfur and fire
'And it rained fire and brimstone.'

No further attestations of Gothic are available on which syntactic analyses may be carried out. The language seems to have vanished without issue.

Not so Old Icelandic, which for this reason deserves more careful investigation.

Although word order in Icelandic was subject to one inviolable constraint, this was not (1) in chapter 1. Rather, the verb in principal clauses of declarative sentences could stand either first or second, but not third, or beyond (Heusler, 1950, 169; Bernstein, n.d., 21). The most frequently attested order, in fact was verb-initial (Heusler, 1950, 173).

Now Old Icelandic, unlike modern Icelandic, was an extremely consistent TYPE B LANGUAGE, a fact that we may demonstrate with some examples.

(i) Pronoun subjects

Even in Old Icelandic, personal pronoun subjects could not be omitted except in poetry (Steblin-Kamensky, 1955, 141). It seems that such deletion was comparatively rare and should probably be dismissed as poetic licence.

In this respect, then, Icelandic behaved like a type A language. We have however defined true type A languages as those which require ALL subject pronouns. In all other languages, Old Icelandic behaved like a true type B language.

(ii) Impersonal verbs

Whether transitive or intransitive, impersonal verbs in Icelandic were usually subjectless. (All examples culled from Heusler, 1950, and Grimm, 1898, IV):

(2) (a) *Rigner.*
      'It is raining.'
  (b) *Várar.*
      'Spring is coming.'
  (c) *Lýste.*
      'It dawned.'

(d)   *Létte   hriþenne.*
      calmed   storm-the (acc.)
      'The storm subsided.'

(e)   *Leysta   ísa.*
      loosed   ice (acc.)
      'The ice broke up.'

(f)   *Af þeim   tok   malet.*
      of   them   took   speech
      'They were left speechless.'

An impersonal passive could be used to express action performed
by an indefinite agent. As in Latin, no superficial subject was
required for this impersonal passive:

(3) (a) *Var   mots   kuatt.*
         was   meeting (dat.)   called
         '*PRO* called to a meeting.'

(b)   *Er   drepet   á   dyrr.*
      is   knocked   at   door
      'There is a knocking at the door.'

(iii) The indefinite agent PRO

Frequently, if not, in fact, usually, this was not spelled out in
active sentences:

(4) (a) *Drepe   þá   á morgen.*
         kill (3 sg. subj.)   them (acc.)   at morning
         'One should kill them in the morning.'

(b)   *Ok   veit   eige   huar   manne   møter.*
      and   knows   not   whether   someone (dat.)   meets
      'And one does not know whether one will meet someone
      or not.'

(c)   *Þarf   eige   at   hugsa   um   þat.*
      may (3 sg.)   not   that   worry (inf.)   about   that
      'One should not worry about that.'

(iv) Extraposition

No dummy subject replaced extraposed sentences:

(5) (a) *Ugger   mik   at   ...*
      worries me (acc.) that
      'It worries me that...'

  (b) *Sýnesk   mér,   at   ...*
      seems   me (dat.) that
      'It seems to me that...'

  (c) *Grunar   mik   at   ...*
      annoys   me (acc.) that
      'It annoys me that...'

As it happens, in each of the examples cited here, the subjectless verb is the first constituent in the clause in which it appears. This was not an unacceptable state of affairs in Old Icelandic, where initial order occurred "so frequently, that it could almost be considered the normal position of the verb" (Heusler, 1950, 173).

In modern, as in Old Icelandic, there are two possible positions of the verb in declarative sentences: verb-initial, suitable for lively narration (Einarsson, 1949, 173) and verb-second, for normal discourse. It is possible that verb-initial order is now more rare than it was in Old Icelandic, but for our purposes, we may consider it to be the sign of a SEPARATE CLAUSE TYPE, as different from the neutral declarative as is, say, the interrogative. In modern Icelandic, the $V/2$ constraint applies only in NEUTRAL declarative sentences.

In German, the rule of *es*-insertion had to be made sensitive to the clause type in which it applied: the rule did not apply to keep the verb in second place in interrogatives, since the $V/2$ constraint is not operative in questions. Similarly, analogous rules in Icelandic will have to be sensitive as to whether or not a clause is declarative or interrogative, but they will also have to be sensitive to a further feature: namely whether the declarative sentence is marked by a special feature, which we may call +*lively*.

Like German, Icelandic is now a type A language, but only insofar as dummy subjects are needed to satisfy the (modified)

$V/2$ constraint. In German, we have seen that *es*-insertion for existential sentences and impersonal passives was sensitive only to word order: in Icelandic, ALL dummy subjects are.

(i) Personal pronoun subjects must, as in Old Icelandic, be present throughout the derivation.

(ii) Impersonal verbs denoting meteorological phenomena are provided with dummy subjects: either *það* (literally, 'that') or *hann* (literally, 'he'). The latter, like personal pronouns in general, can never be deleted, but the presence of the first is subject only to the $V/2$ constraint.

(6) (a) *Það snjóar*
      'It is snowing.'
   (b) *Það hefur verið ágaett upp á siðkastið*
      'It has been excellent weather of late.'

But now consider the following sentences, in which FRONTING has shifted some constituent to the beginning of the sentence:

(7) (a) *Nú snjóar (*það)*
      'Now it is snowing.'
   (b) *Upp á siðkastið hefur (*það) verið ágaett.*
      'Of late it has been excellent weather.'

Similarly, *það* cannot appear in questions, where the verb is free to stand in sentence-initial position:

(8) (a) *Snjóar (*það)?*
      'Is it snowing?'
   (b) *Hefur (*það) verið ágaett upp á siðkastið?*
      'Has it been excellent weather of late?'

The same is true in the case of impersonal middles in modern Icelandic. The impersonal middle construction is used as a possible surface structure realization of the underlying structure *PRO + VP*, and the verb is again supplied with the dummy subject *það:*

(9) (a) *Það er skreiðzt upp á þak.*

it is crept up on roof
'Someone is creeping up on the roof.'

(b) *Það var barizt.*
it was fought
'There was fighting.'

(c) *Það er glaðzt á himnum.*
it is rejoiced in heaven
'There is rejoicing in Heaven.'

But if another constituent has been fronted, and the impersonal
verb thus shifted into second position, the impersonal subject *það*
cannot appear:

(10)(a) *Nú er (*það) skreiðzt upp á þak.*
'Now someone is creeping up on the roof.'

(b) *Hér var (*það) barizt.*
'Here there was fighting.'

(c) *Á himnum er (*það) glaðzt.*
'In Heaven there is rejoicing.'

Conversely, if the verb need not appear in second position anyway,
the dummy pronoun is again obligatorily deleted:

(11)(a) *Er (*það) skreiðzt upp á þak?*
'Is someone creeping up the roof?'

(b) *Var (*það) barizt hér?*
'Was there fighting here?'

(c) *Var (*það) glaðzt á himnum?*
'Was there rejoicing in Heaven?'

(iii) Modern Icelandic has a number of words which can translate
indefinite subjects, among them *maður* (literally, 'man') which most
perfectly approximates German *man*; *folk*, which means what it
seems to; and others. In sentences in which fronting of some non-
subject constituent has applied, these subjects need not be spelled
out:

(12)(a) *Nú   segja   ekki af þeim.*
        now   say (3 pl.) not of them

'They aren't talked about now.'

(b) *Nú segir ekki af þeim.*
now say (3 sg.) not of them
'They aren't talked about now.'

In type A languages as defined by (27) in chapter 4, sentences like (12) should be ungrammatical regardless of word order.

(iv) Dummy subjects to replace extraposed sentences. A pronoun, again *það*, is left behind when subject complements are shifted to the end of the sentence by EXTRAPOSITION:

(13)(a) *Það er réttast, að þér farið heim.*
'It is best that you (sg.) go home.'

(b) *Það er gaman að vera hér.*
'It is fun to be here.'

But when fronting shifts a constituent to the beginning of a sentence in which extraposition has occurred then J*ad* must disappear:

(14)(a) *Nú er (*það) réttast, að þér farið heim.*
'Now it is best for you to go home.'

(b) *Stundum er (*það) gaman að vera hér.*
'Sometimes it is fun to be here.'

The same is true in questions:

(15)(a) *Er (*það) réttast, að þér farið heim?*
'Is it best that you go home?'

(b) *Er (*það) ekki gaman að vera hér?*
'Isn't it fun to be here?'

(v) Existential sentences in modern Icelandic, like their counterparts in German, are marked by subject-verb inversion, and the presence of a dummy sentence-initial pronoun *það:*

(16)(a) *Það voru blöð, blek, og pennar á borðinnu.*
'There were papers, ink, and pens on the table.'

(b) *Það var einu sinnu karl og kerling.*
'There was *(sic)* once an old man and an old woman.'

(c) Það er mjög fallegt útsýni þaðan.
'There is a very beautiful view from there.'

Nevertheless, when fronting has applied in declarative sentences, no það can appear, a fact which by now should occasion the reader no great surprise:

(17) (a) Á borðinnu voru (*það) blöð, blek, og pennar.
'On the table there were papers, ink, and pens.'
(b) Einu sinni var (*það) karl og kerling.
'Once there was an old man and an old woman.'
(c) Þaðan er (*það) mjög fallegt útsýni.
'From there, there is a very beautiful view.'

And the same is true of questions:

(18) (a) Voru (*það) blöð, blek, og pennar á borðinnu?
'Were there papers, ink, and pens, on the table?'
(b) Var (*það) einu sinnu karl og kerling?
'Was there once an old man and an old woman?'
(c) Er (*það) mjög fallegt útsýni?
'Is there a very beautiful view?'

It is seldom that any correlation in linguistics can be so transparently demonstrated, as that between Perlmutter's type A: type B distinction and the word order constraint (1) in chapter 1. Icelandic has undergone two changes in 850 years: first, from being a prominently verb-initial language, it has become a verb-second language. Second, *pari passu*, it has become a type A language: to what extent *pari passu* is demonstrated only too clearly by the sentences (6) through (18).

What does it mean, however, to say that Icelandic is now a type A language? If the presence of the impersonal pronoun það is what identifies Icelandic as such a language, then it is schizophrenic: in declarative sentences where no fronting has occurred, Icelandic is a type A language; in other declarative sentences, and in interrogatives, it is type B. Obviously, the constraint on the presence of subjects is bound entirely to the constraint on the position of the verb.

There is a transformation of *það*-insertion in Icelandic, which like *es*-insertion in German, must be sensitive to the clause type in which it applies. Moreover, as shown by (7), (10), (14), and (17), this rule must be ordered after FRONTING:

(a) fronting
(b) *það*-insertion

For Icelandic to become a true type A language REGARDLESS of word order, it would be sufficient for the ordering of these two rules to be reversed:

(a) *það*-insertion
(b) fronting

Then the presence of the dummy pronoun would not be dependent on the position of the verb, AT LEAST IN SURFACE STRUCTURE.

We have now to turn to some historical evidence from other languages, which demonstrates the existence of such a reordering change.

6

GERMAN

There are only two constructions in modern German where the rule of *es*-insertion seems to be conditioned by word order in surface structure. This same pronoun appears in three other type A constructions quite independently of the position of the verb:

(ii) (a) With weather verbs.
   (b) With impersonal transitive verbs, e.g. *mir graut es* 'I am horrified'.
(iv) With extraposition.

What is interesting about these three constructions is that they have changed since German was first written. We may observe a historical change in progress here, whereby the dummy pronoun, once entirely dependent on the word order constraint, began to appear independently of it.

Old High German, like Old Icelandic, allowed both verb-initial and verb-final order in declarative sentences, with perhaps verb-second order predominating (Lockwood, 1969, 258).

(1) (a) *Want hër do ar arme wuntane bouga.*
   wound he from the arm wound rings
   'From his arm he unwound the coiled rings.'
   (b) *Was liuto filu in flize.*
   was people many in urgency
   'Many people were troubled.'
   (c) *Quimit der brutigomo.*
   'The bridegroom comes.' (source Paul, 1919,71)

(2) (a) *Uber al ist sin geuualt.*
   'Over all is His might.'

(b) *Tho antligita Pilatus.*
     'Then Pilate answered.'
(c) *Min sun bist tu; hiuto gebar ih tih.*
     'My son art thou; today did I bear you.'
(d) *Thanne cumit ther fluobargeist.*
     'Then comes the consoling spirit.'

(source W. Wackernagel, 1835, *passim*)

Given this situation, one would like to find that no subject pronouns were ever required in surface structure. The state of affairs is unfortunately not nearly so obliging, and in a number of cases, impersonal subjects could never be omitted. Possibly the reason for this is that by the time of our earliest texts, verb-second order was already well on the way to becoming generalized.

Yet a careful examination of the three constructions listed will reveal the existence of structurally parallel developments which can most readily be described in terms of a rule reordering.

(ii) (a) Intransitive impersonal verbs

Our discussion of intransitive impersonal verbs, among them those which denote meteorological phenomena, must recognize a division of these into two classes which exhibit slightly different behaviour. On the one hand, we find the true VERBAL predicates, exemplified by such sentences as *es donnert* 'it is thundering'. On the other hand, there are the predicates which consist of the copula and some predicate noun or adjective, illustrated by such examples as *es ist Winter* 'it is winter', and *es ist kalt* 'it is cold'. The difference between the two constructions seems to be purely syntactic: there is no difference in MEANING between OHG *iz abandet* and NHG *es wird Abend*, both of which correctly translate Latin *vesperascit* 'evening is coming'. It is simply an isolated fact about modern German that, unlike Old High German, it no longer has a mono-lexemic inchoative with this meaning.

Yet for some totally unfathomable reason, the behaviour of

these two minimally differentiated constructions was always distinguished with respect to the transformation of *es*-INSERTION.

Even in OHG, impersonal VERBAL predicates required impersonal subjects (Held, 1903, 28; Dal, 1952, 173; Lockwood, 1969, 169). This continues to be the case today.

This was not true of impersonal adjectival and nominal predicates. In OHG, these were free to occur without any impersonal subject (Wilmanns, 1906, 466). Even in MHG, the impersonal subject appeared only in order to keep the verb in second position. If fronting had shifted some other constituent of the sentence to initial position, thereby elbowing the verb into second position, no impersonal subject was attested. Nor was it found in subordinate clauses with verb-final order:

(3) (a) *Ube tag ist, licht ist.*
     'When it is day, it is light.' (from Held, 1903, 28)

   (b) *So heiz wird zi sumere.*
     'It gets so hot in the summers.'
                              (from Wilmanns, 1906, 466)

   (c) *An sinem hove newirdet niemer kalt.*
     'At his court it never gets cold.'
                              (from Wilmanns, 1906, 466)

In modern German, *es*-insertion must again apply where no fronting has occurred:

(4) (a) *Es wird bald Sommer.*
     'It will soon be summer.'

   (b) *Es ist Essenszeit.*
     'It is time to eat.'

But when fronting has shifted the verb into second place, we have two possibilities. The impersonal subject need not appear:

(5) (a) *Bald wird Sommer.*
     'Soon it will be summer.'

   (b) *Nun ist Essenszeit.*
     'Now it is time to eat.'

But it may appear optionally after the verb:

(6) (a) *Bald wird es Sommer.*
'Soon it will be summer.'

   (b) *Nun ist es Essenszeit.*
'Now it is time to eat.'

There is no difference in meaning between (5) and (6): they are distinguished by the application of an optional non-meaning-changing rule.

We postpone a discussion of this rule until we have illustrated this change with some more examples.

(ii) (b) Transitive impersonal verbs

In OHG, transitive impersonal verbs like *limphit* 'behooves' were almost invariably subjectless, whether the resulting position of the verb was sentence-initial (with verb + object order) or second (with object + verb order) (Held, 1903, 30).

VERB + OBJECT ORDER

(7) (a) *Limphit mir.*
'It behooves me.'

   (b) *Tunchet mir reht.*
'It seems right to me.'

   (c) *Gilamf inan.*
'It behooved them.'

OBJECT + VERB ORDER

(8) (a) *Uns limphit.*
'It behooves us.'

   (b) *Mih hungrita.*
'I am hungry.'

   (c) *Mih lusti.*
'I am happy.'

(from Held, 1903, 30; Dal, 1952, 174)

By MHG, a formal subject for such verbs begins to appear intermittently, but "only at the beginning of the sentence" (Lockwood, 1969, 170, cf. Wilmanns, 1906, 469). In Walther, we find:

(9) *Ez troumte ... dem künge...*
     'The king ... dreamed...' (from Walther, 1955, 24)

More significant than the fact that the dummy subject appears only at the beginning of the sentence is that it does so only before the finite verb: no examples are attested in which the verb is moved into THIRD place by the presence of this pronoun, that is, there are no sentences like:

(10) **Es dem künge troumte.*

Held (1903, 56) to whose exemplary summary I owe much of my knowledge and data, recognizes that the presence of *es* is often related to the presence of an object noun phrase, but strangely enough, he does not proceed from there to make what I think are the appropriate conclusions:

...the pronoun is also lacking when the impersonal verb has an object complement. Whether or not inversion (i.e. object-verb inversion: J.H.) takes place, however, seems to be irrelevant.

Thus, he claims that whether the order of constituents in the impersonal sentence is Verb + Object or Object + Verb makes no difference as far as the presence of the impersonal pronoun is concerned. But the very examples which he presents to support his conclusion show the verb always in second position: either the object or some other constituent has been fronted:

(11)(a) *So zimit gotes manne.*
         'So does it behoove a man of God' (Held, 1903, 30)
    (b) *Nu wundert mih dinr grozen wisheit.* (Held, 1903, 56)
         'Now I am amazed at your great wisdom.'
    (c) *Dar umbe wundert mih niht vil.*
         'That doesn't surprise me very much.'(Walther, 1955, 14)

Verb-object inversion (or, more correctly, object-FRONTING) is only ONE of the ways that the verb may be shifted into second place, but it does seem to be the case that *es* (or *ez*) insertion may take place only if other methods of satisfying the *V*/2 constraint have failed.

This is no longer true in modern German. For some verbs of this class, the *es* subject can only appear to prevent verb-initial order:

(12) (a) *Es hungert mich.*
   (b) *Mich hungert (*es).*
      'I am hungry.'
(13) (a) *Es schläfert ihn.*
   (b) *Ihn schläfert (*es).*
      'He is sleepy.'
(14) (a) *Es dünkt mich.*
   (b) *Mich dünkt (*es).*
      'I think', 'Methinks'.

But for a large and CONSTANTLY GROWING number of impersonal transitives, the dummy pronoun *es* can appear after the verb as well as before it:

(15) (a) *Es ekelt mir vor dir.*
   (b) *Mir ekelt ('s) vor dir.*
      'You make me sick.'
(16) (a) *Es verlangt mich nach Speise.*
   (b) *Mich verlangt ('s) nach Speise.*
      'I feel like some food.'
(17) (a) *Es jückt mich.*
   (b) *Mich jückt ('s).*
      'I itch.'
(18) (a) *Es schwindelt mir vor den Augen.*
   (b) *Mir schwindelt ('s) vor den Augen.*
      'I feel dizzy.'

There is no difference in meaning occasioned by the presence or the absence of the impersonal pronoun in the (b) sentences. Moreover, native speakers' judgments are widely at variance as to which verbs allow *es* to appear and which do not. This is exactly what we would expect in observing a change currently in progress, progressing word by word.

(iv) Extraposition

A productive rule in OHG, EXTRAPOSITION often left the finite verb standing at the head of the sentence, and *es*-insertion did not apply:

(19)(a) *War ist, dhaz ...*
         'It is true that...'
   (b) *Ist wunder, daz ...*
         'It is amazing that...'
   (c) *Nu ist offen, thaz ...*
         'Now it is clear that...'

By MHG, with the progressive elimination of verb-initial order, the dummy subject *es* could be lacking only if some other constituent replaced the extraposed sentence at the head of the matrix sentence:

(20)(a) *Dem stüende baz, daz...*
         'It would be better for him, if ...' (Walther, 1955, 16)
   (b) *Groz wunder ist, daz ...*
         'It is remarkable that...' (Walther, 1955, 20)
   (c) *Reht ist, daz...*
         'It is right that...' (Walther, 1955, 80)
   (d) *Dir ist niht kunt, wie...*
         'You do not know how...' (Walther, 1955, 19)

Without fronting, the *es* subject must almost invariably appear:

(21)(a) *Ez ist leider alze lanc, daz ...*
         'Unfortunately, it is all too long (ago), that...'
   (b) *Ez ist reht, daz ...*
         'It is right that...'
   (c) *Ez schinet wol, daz ...*

'It certainly seems that ...'

(from Held, 1903, 103)

In modern German, the situation is somewhat different. In normal word order, *es*-insertion is obligatory, as it seems to have been in MHG:

(22)(a) *Es wäre am besten, heimzugehen.*
         'It would be best to go home.'
    (b) *Es wäre besonders interessant, X festzustellen.*
         'It would be particularly interesting to establish *X*.'
    (c) *Es ist als Grundregel festzuhalten, dass S.*
         'It is to be maintained as a basic principle that *S*.'
    (d) *Es dürfte nicht überflüssig sein, eine Erzählung zu geben.*
         'It may not be superfluous to give an account.'

But in inverted word order, the pronoun *es* may (in some cases, and for some speakers, must) appear:

(23)(a) *Jetzt wäre (es) am besten, heimzukehren.*
         'Now it would be best to go home.'
    (b) *Besonders interessant wäre (es) festzustellen...*
         'It would be particularly interesting to establish...'
    (c) *Als Grundregel ist (es) festzuhalten, dass S.*
         'As a basic principle, it is to be maintained that *S*.'
    (d) *Dagegen dürfte (es) nicht überflüssig sein, eine Erzählung zu geben.*
         'On the other hand, it may not be superfluous to give an account.'

In questions, for example, we might expect that, since there is no $V/2$ target to be satisfied, the appearance of the post-verbal subject pronoun would be optional, yet it does not seem that it could ever be omitted:

(24)(a) *Wäre es am besten, heimzukehren?*
         'Would it be best to go home?'
    (b) *Wäre es nicht interessant, X festzustellen?*
         'Wouldn't it be interesting to establish *X*?'

(c) *Ist es als Grundregel festzuhalten, dass S?*
'Is it to be maintained as a basic principle that *S?*'

(d) *Ist es nicht überflüssig, diese Beispiele zu erwähnen?*
'Isn't it superfluous to mention these examples?'

No explanation will be proposed for the unusual behaviour of these interrogatives in the ensuing discussion. Within the framework of the theory which we assume, the facts of (24) will remain mysterious, but hopefully, not necessarily anomalous.

If we consider only the three constructions herewith described, then *es*-insertion in MHG seems to operate in much the same way as it does in modern German with impersonal passives. That is, given a rule of FRONTING, and another rule of *es*-INSERTION, the two are ordered:

(a) fronting
(b) *es*-insertion

With this ordering, we are able to predict that the introductory pronoun *es* will appear only in sentence-initial position if fronting has failed to apply. We assume that German was a VSO language, and that only FRONTING and *es*-INSERTION could shift the finite verb to second place.

The treatment of these constructions in modern German, on the other hand, does pose certain problems. How are derivations with optional post-verbal *es* to be described?

There are at least three possible derivations, of which the first is hopelessly inadequate, the second implausible, and the third internally consistent, but somewhat paradoxical. We begin with the worst possible derivation, and proceed by stages to a more acceptable solution, by rejecting at each stage the more egregious failings of the previous one.

The first possibility envisages not one rule of *es*-insertion but two, ordered after FRONTING in the derivation of German sentences. The first rule is similar in form to the rule that we have already discussed, and applies obligatorily:

(25) $\# \# \ V \Rightarrow$ es, V
        $(= graut \ mir \Rightarrow es \ graut \ mir$ 'I am horrified')

The second rule is entirely different, and applies optionally:

(26) $\# \# \ Z \ V \Rightarrow Z \ V$ es
        $(= mir \ graut \Rightarrow mir \ graut \ es)$

This solution correctly captures the fact that *es*-insertion is obligatory in sentence-initial position, and optional otherwise for the
constructions under consideration: yet there is an enormous loss
of generality entailed by the claim that there are not one but two
presumably unrelated rules which insert the same semantically
neutral particle.

Fortunately, this unappealing solution can be rejected on purely
empirical grounds: the claim that there are two rules of *es*-insertion
implies that there are grammatical sentences in which both of them
have applied:

(27)   *es graut es mir.*
        'I am horrified.'

There are no such sentences: only one rule of *es*-insertion can apply
within a given sentence. It is possible to capture this fact by putting
an *ad hoc* rider on the second rule of *es*-insertion:

(28) $\# \# \ Z \ V \Rightarrow Z \ V$ es
        (blocked if $Z =$ es)

But an infinitely more satisfactory solution is surely to say that
sentences like (27) are impossible simply because there is only one
rule of *es*-insertion. The problem then is, how this rule is to be
stated?

One possibility is that this rule must precede FRONTING, as was
demonstrated to be the case in existential sentences and impersonal
passives. In that case, the rule would have to be of a different
nature from (25):

(29) $\# \# \ V \Rightarrow V,$ es
        $(= graut \ mir \Rightarrow graut \ es \ mir)$

The subject-like pronoun so generated would now be a possible input for the FRONTING rule. If FRONTING applies to the *es* pronoun, the derivation is complete: *graut es mir* becomes *es graut mir*; if fronting applies to any other constituent, then the dummy subject remains in post-verbal position where it originated: *graut es mir* becomes *mir graut es*. Now a new and optional rule of POST-VERBAL *es*-DELETION may effect a final change: *mir graut es* thereby becomes *mir graut*. The ordering of rules is then:

(a) post-verbal *es* insertion (obligatory)
(b) fronting
(c) post-verbal *es* deletion (optional)

A derivation which incorporates these three rules is in effect a theory that correctly predicts the existence of no more than one *es* in any given sentence. Moreover, the existence of a post-verbal *es*-deletion rule will correctly reflect the fact that the obligatory presence of *es* in surface structure is still dependent on the $V/2$ target. Deletion is only possible if the position of the verb is unaffected thereby.

But this theory is also intuitively unsatisfying in that it violates two previously drawn conclusions about the nature of FRONTING and *es*-INSERTION. Neither of these conclusions, to say the least, can be regarded as sacrosanct: but it is edifying to note that they do reinforce each other.

First is the assumption, stated in chapter one, that fronting is not a totally arbitrary and meaningless rule, but rather one that is correlated with either emphasis, or the topic/comment distinction: only those constituents can be fronted that are either stressed or that resume already available information. The dummy pronoun *es*, like Bach's terminal dummy node Ø, does not qualify as a candidate for FRONTING: therefore, if it stands at the head of the sentence, we must assume, willy-nilly, that it ORIGINATED THERE. Thus, there can be no rule of POST-VERBAL *es*-INSERTION.

This assumption is clearly heretical, in that it violates the cherished assumption that German, at least before FRONTING, is a *VSO* language. Nevertheless, consistent with this heretical assumption is the prediction with which we closed chapter two: that no language like German, with a $V/2$ target, would have a demonstrably oddball rule like *es*-INSERTION which failed to satisfy the target. That is, the rule of *es*-INSERTION could indeed take as its input a sequence $\#\#V$ ..., which violated the $V/2$ constraint, but would have to produce as its output a sequence $\#\#$es V ..., which conformed with that constraint.

Assume that we take these assumptions seriously: an acceptable derivation for impersonal transitives would then have to satisfy the following desiderata:

(a) there is only one rule of *es*-INSERTION
(b) fronting can not apply to meaningless constituents
(c) *es*-insertion must satisfy the $V/2$ target

Such an acceptable derivation exists, but it will be of significantly greater complexity than either of the other two that have been proposed.

Take an input string $\#\#VZ$ (e.g. *graut mir*). To this string, which violates $V/2$, an obligatory rule of pre-verbal *es*-INSERTION now applies:

(30) $\#\#\ V\ Z \Rightarrow$ es, $V\ Z$
        (*graut mir $\Rightarrow$ es graut mir*)

Now a fronting rule may optionally apply to Z. Let us assume that it does, and produces a string $\#\#Z$ es V (* *mir es graut*). The result is a violation of $V/2$, and hence a new and previously unnecessary rule of SUBJECT-VERB INVERSION must apply:

(31) $\#\#Z$ es $V \Rightarrow Z\ V$ es
        (= *mir es graut $\Rightarrow$ mir graut es*)

Now an optional rule of POST-VERBAL *es*-DELETION can produce the terminal string *mir graut*. The order of rules is then:

(a) *es*-insertion (obligatory)
(b) fronting
(c) subject-verb inversion
(d) *es*-deletion (optional)

With the addition of the third of these rules to a derivation of *es*-sentences, we abandon the *VSO* hypothesis, at least for the constructions treated in this chapter. We do so on the basis of no empirical evidence, but only to conform with two intuitively appealing but unproven assertions about the nature of *es*-insertion and FRONTING.

But the *VSO* hypothesis also lacks general empirical confirmation. It was adopted in chapter one on the basis of two constructions in modern German (the existential sentence and the impersonal passive) and on the basis of an uncritically accepted simplicity criterion, which urges that the simplest derivation, or the most general rule, which conforms with a given set of data, must necessarily be the correct one. This criterion will indicate an underlying *VSO* structure for modern German existential sentences, and impersonal passives. It will do the same for Middle High German impersonal transitive sentences, impersonal intransitives with nominal or adjectival predicates, or sentences in which extraposition has occurred.

But it will not do the same for the modern German equivalents of these Middle High German constructions. As we have seen, the assumption that *es*-insertion is a rule that follows FRONTING in these constructions entails the unacceptable conclusion that there are two insertion rules.

What we have demonstrated in this chapter is that for certain constructions WHICH COEXIST SYNCHRONICALLY with *VSO* constructions, the *VSO* hypothesis will fail. We have also shown that the failure of this hypothesis is linked with the appearance of post-verbal *es* in these constructions, and that the appearance of this pronoun in this position is a fairly well attested historical change.

To abandon the *VSO* hypothesis immediately would certainly be premature, however. Instead, we now turn our attention to some more Germanic languages, in order to demonstrate that the phenomenon we have just witnessed in German is not totally an isolated one.

7

OTHER GERMANIC LANGUAGES

Modern Dutch, like modern German, has both the $V/2$ constraint and an impersonal subject *er*, which appears at the beginning of impersonal passives and of existential sentences. Unlike German *es* in these constructions, however, it occurs not only initially, but optionally, post-verbally as well.

Consider the impersonal passives:

(1) (a) *Er wordt geklopt.*
        'There is knocking.'
    (b) *Er wordt hier Hollands gesproken.*
        'Dutch is spoken here.'
    (c) *Er wordt gezongen.*
        'There is singing.'

In each of these, the impersonal subject is all that keeps the finite verb from the beginning of the sentence in which it appears. But the dummy pronoun is not generated only to satisfy a surface structure $V/2$ constraint in declarative sentences. It appears sometimes even in sentences where FRONTING has satisfied the target:

(2) (a) *Hier wordt (er) geklopt.*
        'There is a knocking here.'
    (b) *Hier wordt (er) Hollands gesproken.*
        'Here Dutch is spoken.'
    (c) *Hier wordt (er) gezongen.*
        'Here there is singing.'

And also in sentences where the $V/2$ constraint does not obtain:

(3) (a) *Wordt (er) hier Hollands gesproken?*

'Is Dutch spoken here?'

(b) *Wordt (er) hier gezongen?*
'Is there singing here?'

(c) *Wordt er hier geklopt?*
'Is there a knocking here?'

(4) (a) ... *dat (er) geklopt wordt.*
'... that there is knocking.'

(b) ... *dat (er) hier Hollands gesproken wordt.*
'... that there is Dutch spoken here.'

(c) ... *dat (er) hier gezongen wordt.*
'... that there is singing here.'

With the exception of (3c), optional deletion of post-verbal *er* is always possible in impersonal passives. Yet this pronoun DOES appear, in positions where the *V*/2 constraint would not require it. The same is true of existential sentences, where the impersonal subject must generally appear at the head of the sentence, while the true subject follows the existential verb:

(5) (a) *Er is soms geen boter te krijgen.*
'There is sometimes no butter to be had.'

(b) *Er is hier veel sneeuw.*
'There is much snow here.'

(c) *Er waren tranen in zijn ogen.*
'There were tears in his eyes.'

But unlike German *es* in the parallel construction, Dutch *er* can show up even postverbally, where FRONTING has occurred:

(6) (a) *Soms is (er) geen boter te krijgen.*
'Sometimes there is no butter to be had.'

(b) *Hier is (er) veel sneeuw.*
'Here there is much snow.'

(c) *In zijn ogen waren (er) tranen.*
'In his eyes there were tears.'

The same is true in questions:

(7) (a) *Is (er) geen boter te krijgen?*

'Is there no butter to be had?'

(b) *Is (er) hier veel sneeuw?*
     'Is there much snow here?'

(c) *Waren er tranen in zijn ogen?*
     'Were there tears in his eyes?'

And the dummy subject can also appear in subordinate clauses although the finite verb in these clauses, as in German, must stand at the end of the clause:

(8) (a)   ...*dat (er) hier geen boter te krijgen is.*
          '...that there is no butter to be had here.'

   (b)   ...*dat (er) hier veel sneeuw is.*
          '...that there is much snow here.'

   (c)   ...*dat (er) tranen in zijn ogen waren.*
          '...that there were tears in his eyes.'

In two of the sentences just cited, (3c) and (7c), deletion of post-verbal *er* is blocked. I cannot suggest any reason for this fact, or why it should have been in precisely these sentences, rather than in the other sentences of the (3) and (7) series, that deletion was not allowed to occur. I suspect that there may be a degree of idiosyncrasy involved, and that other informants may have had different judgments from those volunteered by the two that I asked.

But it does seem to me that deletion was LESS LIKELY to occur freely in the (3) and (7) series, than in the others listed here, and thus, that the impossibility of deletion in (3c) and (7c) is not as surprising as would have been, say, the impossibility of such deletion in (2) or (6).

We have already seen in German, that *es*-deletion in post-verbal position is optional for sentences in which extraposition has occurred, but IT IS NOT ALLOWED IN QUESTIONS. (cf. (24) in chapter 6). No explanation was ventured for this fact, and none will be attempted now: but it seems that there may be a hierarchy of constructions, or of syntactic situations, with respect to the freedom with which *es*-deletion may occur: in this hierarchy, which may be language-independent, declarative sentences are 'higher' than questions. If such hierarchies can truly be set up language-independently, their existence confronts us with a genuine puzzle, for there is no conceivable explanation for it within the framework of this discussion. We will return briefly to this matter after some more examples have been presented, not so much because there are answers, as because the existence of a fairly complex hierarchical system of constructions can be fairly definitely established.

A tentative derivation for these constructions in Dutch would be one that included the following ordered rules:

(a) preverbal *er*-insertion (obligatory)
(b) fronting, question formation, or embedding
(c) post-verbal *er*-deletion (optional)

We have just seen that in some circumstances, post-verbal *er*-deletion is no longer optional, but must be blocked.

Let us extrapolate forwards from this situation, and imagine a similar derivation in which the final rule of *er*-deletion is not blocked in only isolated cases, but quite generally: that is, a derivation in which this rule has been dropped entirely from the grammar. In such a derivation, the presence of the dummy pronoun is of course completely independent of the surface structure $V/2$ constraint, and there is no reason whatever to connect the two. This is exactly the situation that prevails in many of the type A languages, with only frozen forms and idioms remaining to show that there was ever any connection between the $V/2$ and the type A constraint. We may illustrate with some examples from Danish, another language with the $V/2$ constraint. Like the other Germanic languages, Danish has an impersonal pronoun (actually TWO, *der* and *det*, which seem to be interchangeable) which occurs in impersonal passives, existential sentences, and in sentences over which extraposition has occurred, as well as the other constructions in which the type A constraint would predict the appearance of such a pronoun. As the original type A constraint predicted, these pronouns must appear regardless of word order:

In impersonal passives:

(9) (a) *Tales der ikke om andet?*
     (b) **Tales —— ikke om andet?*
          'Is nothing else spoken about?'

In existential sentences:

(10)(a) *Her i Byen er der mange rige Folk.*
    (b) **Her i Byen er —— mange rige Folk.*
         'Here in town there are a lot of rich folk.'

In sentences over which extraposition has occurred:

(11)(a) *Nu behøver det ikke at bevises, hvem den skyldige er.*
    (b) **Nu behøver —— ikke at bevises, hvem den skyldige er.*
         'Now it does not need to be proved who was the guilty one.'

Thus in modern Danish, there is virtually nothing to suggest that the presence of the superficial subject has anything to do with word order. I say virtually, because even in the modern language, there are frozen expressions, remnants of happier days, where the subject of the impersonal verb is lacking: all of them are subordinate clauses, where the verb stands at the end of the clause. Both the existence, and the archaic nature of these constructions, suggest that at one time, even in Danish, the impersonal pronoun was needed only in order to keep the verb in second position:

(12)(a) *Hvis muligt er*
         'Whether (it) possible is.'
    (b) *Om saa er*
         'If (it) so is.'
    (c) *Som skik og brug er*
         'As (it) usage and custom is.'
    (d) *Som skrevet er*
         'As (it) written is.'

Most of the modern so-called type A languages (with the exception of the two most familiar, English and French) fall somewhere in between the two extremes illustrated by modern Icelandic and modern Danish respectively. That is, the correlation between word order and the appearance of the dummy pronoun is neither as complete as it is in the former, nor as totally obscured as it is in the latter, of the two cases.

Very close to Icelandic, in both syntax and phonology, is Faroese, which generally provides all impersonal verbs with an impersonal 'subject' *tað:* (source, Lockwood, 1964, 136-137)

(13)(a) *Tað regnar.*
         'It is raining.'
   (b) *Tað blíðkar.*
         'It is getting finer.'
   (c) *Tað døggfellur.*
         'Dew is falling.'
   (d) *Tað gýsur.*
         'It is drafty.'

The same pronoun *tað* also starts existential sentences:

(14)(a) *Tað var einki at gera.*
         'There was nothing to do.'
   (b) *Tað stendur eitt ból uppi á brekkuni.*
         'There is a sheep shelter up on the slope.'

Lockwood points out that the impersonal pronoun "can, as a rule, stand only at the head of the sentence" (1964, 115). In other words, the situation is much as we find it in Icelandic: when an adverb begins the sentence (and the verb consequently is shifted to second place), no *tað* occurs:

(15)(a) *Nú regnar.*
         'Now it is raining.'
   (b) *Nú skýmir.*
         'Now it is getting dark.'
(16)   *Uppi á brekkuni stendur eitt ból.*
         'Up on the slope (there) stands a sheep shelter.'

The same is true for impersonal transitive verbs and impersonal middles, which do require impersonal subjects to occupy the second position in the sentence:

(17)(a) *Honum gekkst væl.*
         'It goes well for him.'

  (b)   *Mær damar.*
         'It seems to me.'

  (c)   *Okkum lukkaðist ikki at fáa seið í dag.*
         (lit. 'to us (it) did not succeed ...')
         'We did not succeed in catching coal-fish today.'

  (d)   *Hart varð rogvið*
         (lit. '(it) was rowed hard')
         'There was hard rowing.'

It appears that the correspondence between word order and the appearance of the subject pronoun *tað* is as complete as it is in Icelandic. Yet in one construction, and one only (with sporadic exceptions), post-verbal *tað* may also appear: with weather verbs, we find not only sentences like (15), but also, and less frequently (Lockwood, 1964, 137) sentences like the following:

(18)   Í *gár regnaði tað.*
        'Yesterday it rained.'

Closer to the Danish extreme, stands modern Swedish. In the earlier attested stages of the language, both the dummy pronoun *det*, and the indefinite agent pronoun *man* needed to appear only at the head of sentences: when an impersonal sentence started with an adverb or with another part of speech than the main verb, generally neither subject appeared (Wessén, 1970, 211, 217).

In modern Swedish, the indefinite agent pronoun *man* can never be omitted; neither in most cases can the impersonal subject pronoun *det*. The only exception noted by Wessén is the class of impersonal transitive verbs, where post-verbal *det* may disappear:

(19)   *Mig synes (det).*
        'It seems to me.'

8

FRENCH AND ENGLISH

Modern English and French are like Danish in that scarcely any traces remain of an original interdependence between the $V/2$ target and the presence of surface structure subject pronouns in sentences. The relationship between the two phenomena is further obliterated moreover, in consequence of the fact that in neither of these languages is there any $V/2$ constraint to be observed.

Accordingly, we must demonstrate that this was not always the case. Our discussion will then be forced to deal with two formally unrelated changes: first, the increasing independence of subject pronouns from the $V/2$ condition; and second the loss of this condition itself. I believe, and will present evidence to suggest, that the two changes are not unrelated in fact. For the moment, however, it is better to treat them separately and postpone discussion of the latter change until we have completed an extremely sketchy summary of the attested behaviour of surface structure pronouns in both French and English.

In French, significantly enough, the impersonal pronouns *il* and *ce* do not even begin to appear in texts until the middle of the twelfth century, the same time that the $V/2$ target was established in surface structure. (Brunot, 1905, 227; Lerch, 1934, 445; Horning, 1880, 247; Gebhardt, 1896, 27-29).

Whether or not the relationship of the two phenomena in question can be clearly established is open to question. Lerch (1934, 455) is the only previous investigator to have suggested that impersonal subjects were, if not introduced, at least generalized, in medieval French specifically in order to keep the finite verb in second position in declarative sentences, but his conjecture seems to be borne out by the data on the whole: most often the impersonal subject appears only at the head of the sentence, in which case it is immediately followed by the verb. If, through FRONTING, another constituent has been preposed, the impersonal pronoun subject is usually lacking.

Thus in sentence-initial position, we find: (source Gebhardt, 1896, *passim*)

(1) (a) *Il en appertenoit au roy.*
           'It behooves the king.'
     (b) *Il le couvient.*
           'It suits him.'
     (c) *Il affiert al crestiente.*
           'It is proper to Christianity.'
     (d) *Il m'est avis encor.*
           'It seems to me yet...'

In sentence-internal position, with these same verbs, we find:

(2) (a) *A votre biaute covandroit.*
           'It would suit your beauty.'
     (b) *A corps humain affiert.*
           'It is proper for the human body.'
     (c) *Bien le m'est avis.*
           'It certainly seems to me.'

In modern French, of course, the impersonal pronoun appears regardless of word order. Yet even now, there remain some more or less frozen expressions in which this pronoun is lacking. Invariably, these expressions are ones which have inverted word order, that is, the subject pronoun, if there were one, would be expected to follow the verb:

(3) (a) *Peu importe* (but cf. *il importe peu*).
           'It matters little.'
     (b) *Peu s'en faut* (but cf. *il s'en faut peu*).
           'Almost.'
     (c) *À Dieu ne plaise* (but cf. *Qu'il ne plaise à Dieu*).
           'Please God.'

(d)   *Si bon vous semblera* (but cf. s'*il* vous semblera bon).
      'If it seems good to you.'

Note: in the last case, we have not inverted word order, but verb-final order in a subordinate clause, as in German.

We may conclude that in medieval French, it is quite likely that impersonal pronouns were inserted by a rule similar to that of *es*-insertion in German:

(4) $\# \; V \Rightarrow il, \; V$

In modern French, the rule that inserts these pronouns does so regardless of word order, and their appearance is no longer confined to sentence-initial position.

Up to this point, our discussion has concerned only the meaningless pronouns, like German *es*, Dutch *er* and French *il*. We have avoided mentioning the personal pronouns not through oversight, but because unlike the impersonal pronouns, their appearance has not been affected by the existence of a $V/2$ target in any of the languages under discussion. They have always appeared in surface structure in such languages as German and Icelandic, and we can observe no historical change in the application of the rule which spells them out. Yet in the type B languages generally, these pronouns, no less than the impersonal pronouns, do not appear in subject position.

For this reason, it is particularly gratifying to see that in medieval French at least, the appearance of subject personal pronouns, like that of impersonal pronouns, was subject to the $V/2$ constraint.

Few investigators have failed to point out that in inverted word order, personal pronoun subjects could be, and usually were, deleted, while in normal word order (i.e. *SVO* order) this was seldom or never the case. (Brunot, 1894, 291; Lerch, 1934, 381; Morf, 1878, 201).

A cursory investigation of the first 100 eligible clauses of the twelfth century *Chanson de Roland* shows that while personal pronoun subjects could never be omitted in *SVO* order, they were eliminated in nine cases out of ten in *VS(O)* order, regardless of person or number:

(5) (a) *Par num d'ocire enveierai (∅) le men.* (st. 3).
          'If he should die, I will send my own son.'
     (b) *Pur quei t'esrages (∅).* (st. 20).
          'Why are you so furious?'
     (c) *Tresqu'en la mer cunquist (∅) la tere altaigne.* (st. 1).
          'He conquered the highland to the sea.'
     (d) *Qui seintes leis tenums (∅).* (st. 32).
          'By whose holy law we abide.'
     (e) *Mult bon plait avreiz (∅).* (st. 6).
          'You will get a very good agreement.'
     (f) *Tant chevalcherent (∅) veies e chemins.* (st. 31).
          'So long did they gallop over highways and byways.'

In the prose and poetry chantefable *Aucassin et Nicolette*, written
perhaps one hundred years later, we find that personal pronoun
subjects in inverted word order could be deleted only about half
the time, while in the prose and poetry of the Renaissance, they
could hardly be deleted at all, except in the most self-consciously
bookish and archaic style:

Dans Rabelais, les récits en langue populaire présentent le pronom sujet
presque toujours exprimé, tandis que les morceaux soignés omettent
avec grande liberté l'emploi de ce même pronom. (Brunot, 1905, 456n).

Thus, there existed in medieval and possibly early modern French,
a rule that deleted subject pronouns after subject-verb agreement:
such a rule applies freely in all the type B languages. In French,
it applied with a very high frequency in those utterances where the
$V/2$ constraint would not, as a result of its application, be violated.
With the passage of time, this deletion rule became ever more
restricted in its application, to disappear almost without a trace
from the grammar of the modern language.

The behaviour of the subject pronouns in English seems to have
been subject to a parallel historical development.

In Old English, or Anglo-Saxon, impersonal verbs of all descriptions frequently lacked the impersonal subject pronoun *hit* 'it'. In

his study of these impersonalia, Wahlén (1925) remarks that there does not seem to have been any hard and fast rule which could predict the appearance of this surface structure pronoun: indeed he laments that the state of things is "next to chaotic", and in the body of his work, specifically refuses to deal with the question any further. Yet before abandoning the subject entirely, he mentions two environments in which the pronoun is almost invariably omitted: in those sentences that are introduced by adverb phrases, and in those that are introduced by an object pronoun (Wahlén, 1925, 9-10). In other words, the pronoun did not appear when the verb stood in second position in the sentence anyway.

This is true not only in the case of subjectless weather verbs, which were really the special object of Wahlén's research, but in two other constructions as well, where modern English has dummy subject pronouns.

As we are aware, a surface structure subject 'it' is required in modern English for sentences over which extraposition of a sentential subject has occurred. This does not seem to have been the case in Old English: at least, not as long as the matrix verb was preceded by another word in the sentence. Consider the following sentences (source Carleton, 1971):

(6) (a) *Her is (∅) on sie swutelung hu Ælfhelm his are and his æhta geuadod hæfð for Gode.*
'It is here in this declaration how Ælfhelm has given his property and his possessions for God.'

(b) *Ða ðuhte us eallen þæt Helmstan moste gan forð.*
'Then (it) seemed to all of us that Helmstan should be permitted to go forth.'

(c) *Gemang þam getidde þæt Myrce gecuran Eadgar to cynge.*
'In the meantime it happened that the Mercians chose Eadgar king.'

In addition, modern English requires a more or less obligatory (and relatively early – i.e. cyclical) rule of *there*-insertion in existential sentences where the subject noun has been moved from the head of the sentence. Again, in Old English, this rule does not seem to have existed, or at least, not to have been obligatory, provided always that no violation of the $V/2$ constraint should arise through the failure of its application.

(7) (a)   *Þises londes earan ðrie sulong.*
          'Of this land there are three sulongs.'
    (b)   *And þissera gewritu syndan þreo.*
          'And there are three of these declarations.'

Not only the impersonal pronoun *hit*, but even the indefinite agent pronoun *man* could be omitted, subject to the same conditions as the other (Pogatscher, 1901, 295):

(8)   *Nu mæz (∅) cunnian hwa cene sy...*
          'Now one should find out who is valiant...'

Personal pronoun subjects were also frequently deleted in subordinate clauses, which were marked by verb-final order (Pogatscher, 1901, 272). This too is what could be expected if the subject pronoun were spelled out in surface structure only to satisfy the $V/2$ target in Old English.

The optionality of impersonal pronoun subjects at least survives to some degree even in medieval English, as we can convince ourselves by considering the more or less familiar utterances:

(9) (a)   Thee availeth not to cry.
    (b)   Methought the wood began to move.
    (c)   And therefore the(e) behoueth now to chese.
    (d)   Me longeth sore to bernysdale.
    (e)   To thee pertains to do the Lord's command.

                                        (source Spies, 1901, 53)

TWO SYNTACTIC CHANGES

Fragmentary though it is, the foregoing summary has provided us with evidence for at least two changes in the type A languages under discussion.

Change 1

Originally, the impersonal pronoun is inserted by a rule that follows the application of the fronting rule. This is still true of *es*-insertion in two constructions in German, and was presumably true of the rules that inserted subject *il* in French, and subject *hit* in Old English. In modern Icelandic, all cases of *það* insertion in surface structure are provided for by such a rule.

Later, in German, Dutch, French, Danish, Swedish and English, the impersonal pronoun is inserted by a rule that must in any event PRECEDE the fronting rule. We may then speak of two stages that we may call (with malice aforethought) stages 0 and 2, respectively:

Stage 0	*Stage* 2
(a) fronting	(a) $\# \ V \Rightarrow \# $ pronoun, V
(b) $\# \ V \Rightarrow \# $ pronoun, V	(b) fronting
	(c) subject-verb inversion
	(d) V pronoun $\Rightarrow V \emptyset$ (optional)

Note that stage 2 requires not only a reversal in the order of application of fronting and pronoun insertion, but in addition a wholly new and as yet unmotivated rule of subject-verb inversion.

Justification for such a rule is soon forthcoming: we postpone it very briefly now to illustrate

Change 2

The fourth rule of stage two, the rule which deletes post-verbal impersonal and other pronouns becomes ever more restricted and finally ceases to operate at all. This change is attested in the case of personal pronouns, by French; in the case of impersonal pronouns, by German, Dutch, and Danish, as well as French. We may then talk of a stage three which follows stage two:

Stage 2	*Stage* 3
(a) $\# \ V \Rightarrow \#$ pronoun, V	(a) $\# \ V \Rightarrow \#$ pronoun, V
(b) fronting	(b) fronting
(c) subject-verb inversion	(c) subject-verb inversion
(d) V pronoun $\Rightarrow V \emptyset$	(d) ———
(optional)	(the rule is dropped)

Change two exemplifies a common historical process in language change: a low level rule, through successively greater limitations on its application, is dropped from the grammar of a language.

Extrapolating backwards from stages 3 and 2, we can envision an earlier stage (which we can call stage 1) in which the final rule is neither dropped, as in stage 3, or optional, as in stage 2, but unrestricted and obligatory:

Stage 1

(a) $\# \ V \Rightarrow \#$ pronoun, V
(b) fronting
(c) subject-verb inversion
(d) V pronoun $\Rightarrow V \emptyset$ (obligatory)

Is this stage ever historically attested?

For personal pronouns, it is, or almost is, in French as recorded in the *Chanson de Roland*. Personal pronouns are presumably available in deep structure as meaning-bearing elements. If they are absent in post-verbal position, as in this work they almost invariably are, it must be by the operation of a deletion rule which, if not obligatory, admits only a few exceptions.

But it is literally impossible to find any attestation for a stage 1 with dummy pronouns in any of the languages that we have so far described, for the reason that this stage is functionally equivalent to the much simpler stage 0:

Stage 0	*Stage* 1
(a) fronting	(a) $\# \ V \Rightarrow \# $ pronoun, V
(b) $\# \ V \Rightarrow \# $ pronoun, V	(b) fronting
	(c) subject-verb inversion
	(d) V pronoun $\Rightarrow V \emptyset$ (obligatory)

As we have tried to show in the first part of this study, the simplest and most revealing description of *es*-insertion in German existential sentences and impersonal passives is a derivation which approximates stage 0; the alternative, a derivation like that illustrated by stage one, would fail to reflect the fact that the pronoun in question is generated only in order to satisfy the $V/2$ target.

Yet the 'psychological reality' of a stage one is a different question entirely. Whether or not stage 0 ever enjoyed any 'psychological reality', there can be no doubt that at some point it was reinterpreted as stage 1 in the grammars of the speakers of German and Dutch. The reason is this: both stage 2, and a subsequent change from stage 2 to stage 3 are well attested. Both of these involve a low-level deletion rule, the rule (d). In stage 0, which demonstrably precedes stage two, THERE IS NO SUCH RULE IN THE DERIVATION. It is impossible to delete a low-level rule which is not there.

In order for the rule

(1) V pronoun $\Rightarrow$ $V \emptyset$

to exist, stage 0 must have been replaced by the more cumbersome stage 1, a derivation in which this rule is included.

Fortunately, we need not take the existence of a stage 1 entirely on trust. In one type A language, Romansh, we have actual morphological evidence for the existence of such a derivation.

There can be no evidence in the Germanic languages that stage 1 actually had an autonomous existence of its own. But in the Surselvan dialect of Romansh, we are fortunate in being able to observe a stage 1 derivation as distinct from a stage 0 derivation: that is, there are some sentences which in their derivation, must include a rule of impersonal pronoun insertion and a subsequent rule of pronoun deletion.

We owe the opportunity to observe this unusual derivation to the fact that Surselvan, unlike the other languages with a $V/2$ target, has predicate adjectives which must agree with the subject for the feature of gender. There are three phonologically distinct predicate adjective endings:

masculine -*s*
feminine -*a*
neutre   -*$\emptyset$*

All nouns in Surselvan, however, are either masculine or feminine. In all, there are only three possible subjects which may take neutre predicate adjective concord. They are

(α) sentential subjects,
(β) the demonstrative pronoun *quei*,
(γ) the impersonal pronoun *igl* 'it'.

We may illustrate each of these cases with some examples.

(α) Sentential subjects

(2)   *Ch'ins se gidi l'in l'auter ei bien e bi.*
        'To help one another is good and beautiful.'

Compare with this the equally vapid but illustrative sentence

(3)   *L'uffaun ei buns e bials.*
        'The child (masculine) is good and beautiful.'

Note that not only the characteristic -*s*-ending, but also a different vowel in the root distinguishes the masculine form. This distinction, which involves only a small number of adjectives seems to result from the fact that the original neutre ending, but not the masculine, caused *umlaut* in the preceding vowel. Fortunately, the phonology of this need not concern us; the example is useful in that it illustrates beyond any doubt that the contrast between the masculine and neutre forms is considerable.

(β)   The demonstrative pronoun *quei*

(4)   *Quei ei stau ferm tubac.*
        'That was strong tobacco.'

Compare with this,

(5)   *Il tubac ei staus ferms.*
        'The tobacco was strong.'

Note that the adjective *ferm* 'strong' takes the masculine -*s* ending only when it is a predicate adjective: in the attributive, no such ending is ever found, with the consequence that the masculine attributive adjective is identical with the neutre predicative form. The past participle *stau(s)*, on the other hand, is in both (4) and (5) a predicate adjective, and the difference between the two forms follows from the fact that in the first sentence, concord is with the neutre pronoun *quei* 'that', and in the second with the masculine noun *tubac* 'tobacco'.

(γ)   The impersonal pronoun *igl*

(6) (a)   *Igl ei sesalzau in urezi.*
           'There arose a storm.'
    (b)   *Igl ei vegniu in giuvnatsch alla radunonza.*
           'There came to the meeting a churl.'

    (c)   *Igl ei stau mo in fiug in questa val.*
          'There was only one fire in this valley.'

Compare with these:

(7) (a) *In urezi ei sesalzaus.*
         'A storm arose.'
    (b) *In giuvnatsch ei vegnius alla radunonza.*
        'A churl came to the meeting.'
    (c) *Mo in fiug ei staus emblidaus in qesta val.*
        'Only one fire was forgotten (untended) in this valley.'

Igl-insertion in Surselvan takes place almost as freely as does *es*-insertion in German. Being at a loss for defining exactly what the constraints on its application may be, I will content myself with pointing out a few sentences in which *igl*-insertion is, if not quite ungrammatical, at least terribly awkward:

(8) (a) *??Igl ei sedustau cun tapfradad il schuldau.*
         'There defended himself valiantly the soldier.'
    (b) *??Igl ei emblidau la fiasta il parsun.*
        'There forgot the party the treasurer.'
    (c) **Igl ei vegniu alla radunonza el.*
        'There came to the meeting he.'

Now Romansh, as we have noted, is a $V/2$ language. If FRONTING applies in any of the sentences of (6) and the $V/2$ target is thus satisfied, the neutre pronoun *igl* cannot overtly appear:

(9) (a) *Suenter mezdi ei sesalzau in urezi.*
         'After noon there arose a storm.'
    (b) *Alla radunonza ei vegniu in giuvnatsch.*
        'To the meeting there came a churl.'
    (c) *In questa val ei stau mo in fiug.*
        'In this valley there was only one fire.'

If fronting is applied to the sentences of (7), the resulting sentences are different:

(10) (a) *Suenter mezdi ei in urezi sesalzaus.*
      'After noon a storm arose.'

  (b) *Alla radunonza ei in giuvnatsch vegnius.*
      'To the meeting came a churl.'

  (c) *In questa val ei mo in fiug staus emblidaus.*
      'In this valley only one fire was forgotten.'

The sentences (9) and (10) differ in that the predicate adjective in the former, but not in the latter, has neutre concord: this in spite of the fact that there is no neutre pronoun *igl* present in the surface structure of the sentences of (9). I propose that in these sentences, the pronoun is deleted after predicate adjective gender agreement has taken place.

Needless to say, another explanation is possible, and must be demonstrated false.

The sentences (9) and (10) differ in word order: in the former, the true subject FOLLOWS the predicate past participle while in the latter, it PRECEDES this participle. It may plausibly be argued that the predicate adjective will agree with the subject noun only if the latter precedes it in the sentence: thus, the neutre form of the past participle in (9) is to be explained by word order alone, and not by appealing to some deleted neutre pronoun *igl*.

It can easily be shown, by considering a few more sentences, that the word order explanation is misguided. Predicate adjectives may be subject to the fronting rule in Surselvan, with the result that the subject noun will follow its predicate adjective. Yet this adjective will still agree with the following noun in number and gender:

(11) (a) *Bialas sun las flurs da sta.*
      'Beautiful (feminine plural) are the flowers (feminine plural) of summer.'

  (b) *Sgarscheivla ei la paupradad.*
      'Wretched (fem. sg.) is poverty (fem. sg.).'

It may then be argued that gender agreement is ordered before FRONTING, but in all other respects is a surface structure rule sensitive to word order only. Even this *ad hoc* and desperate solution will not work, if only because it overlooks an extremely important generalization about grammaticality.

As we have noted, not all sentences allow *igl*-insertion. By the same token, not all sentences of the type (9) are grammatical. In fact, they are respectively awkward or ungrammatical under EXACTLY THE SAME circumstances that *igl*-insertion is awkward or ungrammatical:

(12)(a) *?Cun tapfradad ei se̲du̲s̲t̲au il schuldau.*
         'With valour defended himself the soldier.'
   (b)   *?La fiasta ei e̲m̲b̲l̲i̲d̲au il parsun.*
         'The party forgot the treasurer.'
   (c)   **Alla radunonza ei v̲e̲g̲n̲iu el.*
         'To the meeting came he.'

All of these sentences are perfectly unexceptionable with masculine predicate adjectives:

(13)(a) *Cun tapfradad ei il schuldau se̲du̲s̲t̲aus.*
         'With valour the soldier defended himself.'
   (b)   *La fiasta ei il parsun e̲m̲b̲l̲i̲d̲au.*
         'The treasurer forgot the party.'
   (c)   *Alla radunonza eis el v̲e̲g̲n̲ius.*
         'He came to the meeting.'

In the face of this evidence, to claim that *igl*-insertion did not take place in (9) is virtually indefensible.

The derivation of those sentences must therefore include the following ordered rules:

(14)(a) *igl*-insertion
   (b)   subject-predicate gender agreement
   (c)   fronting
   (d)   subject-verb inversion
   (e)   *igl*-deletion.

We include a sample derivation for (9a):

ei sesalzau in urezi suenter mezdi (initial string) ⇒

igl ei sesalzau in urezi suenter mezdi (*igl*-insertion) ⇒
igl ei sesalzau in urezi suenter mezdi (agreement) ⇒
suenter mezdi igl ei sesalzau in urezi (fronting) ⇒
suenter mezdi ei igl sesalzau in urezi (subject-verb inversion) ⇒
suenter mezdi ei sesalzau in urezi. (*igl*-deletion)

Even if we ignore the morphological evidence of Surselvan, evidence which for the Germanic languages is perhaps primarily anecdotal, we are forced to recognize the existence of stage 1 as the necessary precursor to the amply attested stage 2. The question then, is this: why did a change, such as the one that we postulate must have converted stage 1 into stage 2, occur at all?

As a first, and totally inadequate, approximation to an answer to this question, I propose the following possible mechanism of syntactic change:

(15)   Rules which spell out subject pronouns will tend to appear ever earlier in derivations.

To comply with this tendency, we suggest that derivations may even be complicated by the addition of a new rule such as subject-verb inversion. It is to the motivation for this rule that we must now finally address ourselves.

There are, among others, two ways of describing word order in German sentences: the first is to do as we have done in part one, positing *VSO* order as basic, and deriving all other configurations from this, whether *SVO* or *ZVS*, by the application of the FRONTING rule. As I have tried to demonstrate, this derivation for two constructions at least has the merit of simplicity.

A second way of accounting for the order of words in declarative sentences is to posit an underlying *SVO* order, and then derive *ZVS* from this order by the successive application of the FRONTING rule and a rule of subject-verb inversion. Explicitly in recent (i.e. transformational) descriptions, and implicitly in traditional analyses, which speak of 'inversion', this is the framework within which all grammarians, whether native or otherwise, have chosen to describe German, presumably for a reason: *SVO* order is what corresponds to their intuitions. Here at least is one case where these intuitions must be respected, for there is other, historical evidence which tends to substantiate the correctness of the *SVO* analysis. We turn now to an investigation of the process whereby French and English both lost the $V/2$ target, and illustrate how this change provides evidence for a rule of subject-verb inversion in $V/2$ languages in general.

In French, the $V/2$ target was still maintained in the prose of Froissart's Chronicles, but already there were signs of impending attrition. In some cases where topicalization preposed a constituent other than the subject, subject-verb inversion regularly failed to occur, with the result that the verb was left as the third constituent in the sentence in which fronting had occurred. This was regularly the case when the preposed constituent was an object noun phrase, and the subject, a personal pronoun. (Ebering, 1881, 349).

By the seventeenth century, subject-verb inversion after fronting in declarative sentences was apparently an optional rule which seems to have applied about half the time (Brunot, 1909, 664-669), and in modern French, as we know, it no longer takes place at all, except in some archaic expressions, and regularly with a small class of introductory adverbs like *aussi* 'therefore' and *encore* 'yet'. The loss of subject-verb inversion is the only reason for the failure of modern French to satisfy the $V/2$ target even today.

Word order in medieval and old English was never so rigidly constrained as in French, to say nothing of modern German, yet the general validity of a $V/2$ constraint seems to be reasonably clear.

By the fourteenth century, subject-verb inversion was breaking down, leaving the subject noun phrase in second, and the main verb in third position in the sentence. Swieczkowski (1962) in a study of word order in the poetry and prose of the period, reports that in Langland's *Piers the Plowman*, subject-verb inversion after FRONTING takes place about half the time, whereas in the prose sermons of the same period, under the same conditions, subject-verb inversion occurs only one time out of four.

In modern English, as in modern French, subject-verb inversion seems to apply only when the so-called AFFECTIVE words introduce the sentence. Otherwise, the rule has been dropped. As is true of French, this is the only factor that stands in the way of English being a $V/2$ language today.

With $V/3$ order possible in declarative sentences, there is not the same reason for considering English and French to be VSO languages as we can cite for the $V/2$ languages. If we then assume that these two languages have a SVO base, we can talk of two stages in their historical development, stages which once again we can designate by number:

Stage 2	*Stage* 3
(a) fronting	(a) fronting
(b) subject-verb inversion	(b) ———
(optional)	(the rule is dropped)

The first of these stages describes medieval English and French with respect to the phenomenon of word order; the second describes the modern languages.

Once more, given stages 2 and 3 in a historical development, we are able to extrapolate backwards to an earlier stage one, where the subject-verb inversion rule is not optional but obligatory and unrestricted in its application.

Stage 1

(a) fronting
(b) subject-verb inversion
(obligatory)

The reader can easily verify for himself that a language with an SVO base, and the rules of fronting and subject-verb inversion as outlined in stage three will be a $V/2$ language.

As we have shown, the simplest description for a $V/2$ language is one that posits underlying VSO order and no rule of subject-verb inversion. For this reason, we can find no independently attested stage one with respect to this transformation, since any language which included in its derivations the obligatory application of the rule, would theoretically be at a stage 0, with *VSO* order, and need no such rule whatever.

Yet we must assume that if stage 0 ever had any psychological reality whatever, it must have been reinterpreted as the functionally equivalent stage 1:

Stage 0: *VSO* order	*Stage* 1: *SVO* order
(a) fronting	(a) fronting
	(b) subject-verb inversion (obligatory)

The reason that such a reinterpretation must have taken place in French and English while they were *V/2* languages is that both the well-attested stages two and three presuppose underlying *SVO* word order and the existence of a low-level rule of subject-verb inversion, and the evidence is quite clear that stage 2 succeeded stage 0. Yet in stage 0 there is no low-level rule of subject-verb inversion, whose application could be curtailed until it dropped from the grammar.

We thus argue for the existence of what are affectively two reinterpretations, between a hypothetical stage 0 and a succeeding, and functionally equivalent, stage 1. The two changes which are embodied in the transition from one to the other, namely:

Stage 0	*Stage* 1
(a) fronting subject pronoun insertion	(a) subject pronoun insertion fronting
(b) *VSO* base order	(b) *SVO* order

are essentially separate, although they are clearly related, as we can see by comparing the derivations as a whole:

Stage 0: *VSO*	*Stage* 1: *SVO*

(a) fronting   (a) $\# V \Rightarrow \#$ pronoun, V
(b) $\# V \Rightarrow \#$ pronoun, V (b) fronting
                            (c) subject-verb inversion

It has been a truism of theories of grammatical change that the restructuring of a grammatical system from one generation to the next will proceed in the direction of greater simplicity. One of the first examples in transformational literature of such a demonstrable change is Kiparsky's (1965) account of the phonological restructuring that attended, and followed the working of Grimm's Law in the Germanic languages, but this example is by no means the only one.

Plainly, a transition from stage 0 as we have pictured it to a functionally equivalent stage 1, a derivation of greater complexity, contravenes this otherwise well-attested tendency, and we should try, if possible, to find a satisfactory explanation, or at least a general principle, which allows such a change to occur.

What is common to both of the reinterpretations that we have outlined is that they eliminate verb-initial order BEFORE the application of the fronting rule, one by moving the real subject (if there is one), and the other by inserting the dummy pronoun, at the head of the sentence. The effective result of these operations is that the $V/2$ target is satisfied not only in surface syntactic structure, that is, following the application of all syntactic transformations, but at a more remote level as well, in fact, the level, if it may be so called, that precedes the application of the FRONTING rule.

Does this level have any systematic significance? We know that FRONTING is a post-cyclical rule; furthermore, I know of no other post-cyclical rules that would have to precede PRONOUN INSERTION in a stage 1 derivation. We may therefore propose the hypothesis that

(16)   In stage 1, $V/2$ is a shallow structure target, where shallow
         structure is defined as the level that results upon the

application of all the rules in the cycle, but none of the post-cyclical rules.

If this is so, English and French satisfy the $V/2$ target at the shallow structure level only; other languages like Dutch and Danish do so in both shallow structure and surface structure; German is $V/2$ in surface structure and, in all constructions but the impersonal passive and the existential sentence, in shallow structure as well; and Icelandic and Faroese are $V/2$ in surface structure only.

A possible mechanism of syntactic change is then that

(17)   Targets will be satisfied at earlier and earlier stages in the derivation of sentences, that is, ever closer to deep structure.

A formulation such as the above, while it may serve as a convenient summary for a number of related changes, is nevertheless by itself no explanation for these changes: on the contrary, it stands in need of some explanation itself.

Almost no work has been done in the field of syntactic change, but phonological change has been more extensively investigated, and, as it happens, two theories have been proposed that are not irrelevant to the Germanic developments that are outlined in this study.

In conclusion, I would like to present these theories and indicate briefly how they may help us understand the nature of certain syntactic changes.

One component of the target-movement process, as we have seen, is a reordering of the application of two rules. Starting with an ordering relationship

(a) fronting
(b) *es*-insertion

in most sentence types, German, and the Germanic languages, now have an ordering relationship between these two rules that is the opposite of the one started with, namely

(a) *es*-insertion

(b) fronting
(c) subject-verb inversion.

The situation is reminiscent of one that is discussed at length in Kiparsky (1968). In the first case, which corresponds to stage 1, fronting applies to *VSO* structures and creates derived structures to which the rule of *es*-insertion, by virtue of its structural index, can no longer apply. The rules are thus in a BLEEDING relationship. Kiparsky has argued that bleeding relationships of this sort will tend to be eliminated, or, more generally, that rules will shift into the order that allows their fullest utilization in the grammar. This is, of course, the order that we find in the second case, which corresponds to stage 1: here, *es*-insertion will apply in all sentences, not only those in which FRONTING has failed to apply.

We might therefore be tempted to say that the diachronic rule reordering discussed above is simply a syntactic example of a universal tendency described for phonological derivations. Yet this explanation, for all its plausibility, is at the very least incomplete. Like the earlier principle (15), it will account at best for only one of two related changes.

Another change, which led to the loss of the *V*/2 target in French and English, is the replacement of *VSO* by *SVO* as the underlying order of constituents in these languages while they were still surface structure *V*/2 languages. This change may not have proceeded *pari passu* with the rule reordering discussed above. Yet the mechanism by which it was effected, and the stages of its development, are so similar to the changes involving *es*-insertion, that to overlook their similarity and to try to find different explanations for the two is surely to miss a significant generalization.

We have suggested that the relevant generalization linking these two changes is that the *V*/2 target 'went underground': the reordering of *es*-insertion and the creation of a new underlying *SVO* order are both aspects of this fact.

It is evident that the change *VSO* to *SVO* cannot have had anything to do with the principle of reordering rules to allow for their maximum utilization. If the two changes that pushed the target underground are to be discussed and explained together, then rule reordering will scarcely provide the necessary common bond.

A possible explanation with the required generality is suggested in Hale (1971), where a variety of phonological restructurings are discussed. The essential thesis of his work is this: if a constraint on canonical forms exists in surface structure, then there will be a tendency to interpret the underlying forms to which the grammatical rules apply in such a fashion that these forms too will be subject to the surface structure constraint.

An excellent example is furnished by Maori, whose morphemes are subject to the surface structure constraint that they end in a vowel. There are apparently no exceptions to this constraint.

In a number of cases, it makes for very simple and elegant derivations to posit UNDERLYING consonant-final forms for verb roots, and include in the grammar a general rule deleting word-final consonants, but not morpheme-final consonants that are followed by vocalic roots. The alternative is to allow a proliferation of unpredictable alternate suffix forms. And yet, a variety of facts suggest that the latter is the true situation in Maori. As a result, the grammar of the verbal morphology is vastly complicated, but there is no disparity between the canonical surface structure forms and the underlying forms from which they are derived: in deep structure, as in surface structure, all morphemes end in vowels.

Possibly a similar process is at work in the syntactic examples under discussion here. In surface structure, the $V/2$ target is a constraint on canonical sentence types: the simplest derivation that will produce these forms is one that proceeds from an underlying order VSO, in which this constraint is naturally not observed. The disparity between deep and shallow structure is eliminated when SVO order is found in shallow structure, and es-insertion (and its analogues in the other type A languages) is allowed to precede FRONTING. The result is a cumbersome derivation which includes a hitherto unnecessary rule, but apparently the price is not an excessive one to pay for being able to 'hug the syntactic ground'.

Given that the goal of such a reinterpretation process is to eliminate disparities between canonical DEEP and surface forms, we would expect to find that the rules of dummy pronoun insertion would begin to apply within the cycle itself.

As we know, this is the case with the English pronouns *it* and *there*, both of which must be generated by cyclic rules, and which in turn may be the input to further cyclic rules, such as subject-raising and passivization. In English, these pronouns may no longer be deleted even when they are no longer the subject of verbs marked for tense. Thus:

(18)(a) I expect it to rain
    (b) I expect there to be no trouble.

Other languages like French and German, have not yet gone so far:

(19)(a) *Dieu laisse pleuvoir.*
        'God lets (it) rain.'
    (b) *Gott lässt regnen.*
        'God lets it rain.'

The simplest derivation for these sentences is one that calls for insertion of the dummy pronoun at the shallow structure level only. An alternative derivation of greater complexity would include a cyclical insertion rule, followed by an obligatory deletion rule if the subject pronoun is no longer the subject of a finite verb. When, in time, this deletion rule becomes OPTIONAL, as it already seems to be doing in some dialects, it will be a sign that the target has dug itself even deeper by a process of reinterpretation similar to the one that has been outlined above:

(20)(a) *Dieu (le) laisse pleuvoir.*
    (b) *Got lässt (es) regnen.*

Of these, the German is now unexceptionable, while the French is still substandard: but who knows what the future will bring?

TABLE 1

A Summary of the Proposed Changes[a]

(1) Loss of verb-final order in the Germanic languages.

(2) The genesis of the $V/2$ target with *es*-insertion.

(3) Dummy pronoun forms begin to appear OPTIONALLY in positions where the $V/2$ target does not require them.

(4) The dummy pronoun begins to appear OBLIGATORILY in positions where the $V/2$ target does not require it.

(5) Underlying *VSO* order is reinterpreted as underlying *SVO* prior to the FRONTING rule.

(6) Subject-verb inversion becomes optional following FRONTING.

(7) The rule of subject-verb inversion is dropped from the grammar of the language.

(8) In some languages, dummy pronoun insertion rules begin to apply within the cycle itself, with no possibility of subsequent deletion.

[a] not all of these changes are strictly ordered with reference to every other: in particular, there is no reason to suppose that change (5) must follow change (4).

EPILOGUE ON SOME UNANSWERED QUESTIONS

1. Hierarchies of Constructions

In chapter 7, it was mentioned that there seemed to exist a hierarchy of constructions which could be ranked with respect to the freedom with which they permit deletion of the post-verbal dummy pronoun. I suggested there that probably deletion of the post-verbal dummy pronouns *es* in German and *er* in Dutch could occur more freely in declaratives than in interrogatives. More generally, of the constructions which, in *V*/2 languages, require dummy subjects, some will be less apt than others to permit deletion of these subjects under any circumstances whatever. For ease of reference, these constructions are presented here once more:

(i)   impersonal verbs
    (a)   intransitive *(es regnet)*
    (b)   transitive *(es graut mir)*
    (c)   passive or middle *(es wurde getanzt)*
(ii) extraposed sentences
(iii) existential sentences

There are in addition, the meaning bearing pronouns which can be omitted from subject position in many languages, but never from the *V*/2 languages:

(iv) the indefinite agent pronouns (man)
(v)   the personal pronouns

In Perlmutter (1968) it was claimed that in all type A languages, the pronoun subjects would have to appear in all the 7 situations described above. We have shown in this study that no really clear-cut distinction exists between the 'type A' languages and other languages, and that, with the passage of time, languages close to a 'type B' standard may evolve into 'type A' languages by degrees. In fact, there are stages, attested for individual languages, when the given language may be 'type A' with respect to the deletability of personal pronoun subjects, but 'type B' with respect to the deletability of personal pronoun subjects in existential sentences.

For purposes of the following discussion, it is preferable to abandon the type A: type B distinction as imprecise, and substitute instead stage 1, (= stage 0) stage 2, and stage 3, where stage 1 is closest to type B (that is, the pronoun is necessary in surface structure, but only in order to keep the verb in second place), stage three more or less equivalent to type A (the pronoun is always needed) and stage two intermediate between the two.

Old High German, as far as our records indicate, was always at stage three for constructions (ia), (iv), and (v). Modern German, on the other hand, is still at stage one for constructions (ic) and (iii), and at stage two for (ib) and (ii). We may note that even such a construction as (ia) has not survived the years unchanged: while even as late as early modern German, the subject of weather verbs was not inserted in the cycle itself, in some dialects of modern German it now is, as we can see from (20b) in chapter 9. We may talk, rather imprecisely, of a stage beyond stage 3, and note that, significantly enough, it is only (ia) which has entered this stage in German.

Ignoring the meaning-bearing pronouns (iv) and (v), we can establish a hierarchy of the constructions in German which use the dummy pronoun *es*, according to the degree to which they have advanced from stage one, or a complete dependency on the $V/2$ constraint. From most advanced to least advanced, they are:

E.1 (ia)
(ib), (ii)
(ic), (iii)

In itself, this hierarchy is of no particular interest. What redeems it is the fact that it does not seem to be confined in its validity to German. Insofar as there are any differences among constructions in the other $V/2$ languages, those differences only tend to confirm exactly this hierarchy.

For example, in Dutch, only (ic) and (iii) are still at stage 2: all constructions higher on the hierarchy are at stage 3. In modern Faroese, all constructions but (ia) are at stage 1, but (ia) is entering into stage 2. In Old Swedish, both (ia) and (ib) were stage two, but now the former is at stage 3.

I suspect that more intensive research into any of these languages and their history will tend to confirm further the existence of the hierarchy E.1.

Quite needless to say, no explanation is available at this time for the existence of such a hierarchy as E.1. It is presented as a puzzle in search of a solution.

2. Why not Gronk insertion

In part I, it was claimed that a rule of the form

$$\text{E.2} \quad \# V \Rightarrow \# \text{ es, } V$$

existed only in order to satisfy the $V/2$ constraint, and thus, implicitly, that any linguistic element whatsoever could be chosen as the place-filling item. And yet, in all the other $V/2$ languages under discussion, the inserted article was either a neutre pronoun, like Danish *det*, or an adverbial pronoun, like Dutch *er* or English *there*. More disconcertingly perhaps, a number of non-$V/2$ languages have similar subject pronouns.

Miklosich (1883, 5) points out that in some Slovenian dialects, impersonal subjects are sporadically found for impersonal verbs, and rightly or wrongly, attributes their appearance to German influence. On the other hand, Horning (1880, 261-262) shows that impersonal pronoun subjects are also sometimes found in varieties of Italian, Spanish and Portuguese, in which it would be vain to look for any Germanic influence.

This is a fact that cannot be explained by reference to purely structural conditions like the existence of a $V/2$ target: the best we can claim is that a result of this condition, a sporadic and structurally insignificant feature of a language may become, as it were, canonized.

Why this feature should exist at all is a question which we leave out of this study, having nothing more cogent to suggest than the animistic speculations that have bedeviled so much of the previous research on this entire topic.

3. Why not Greek

In his classic study of clitics and word order in Indo-European dialects, J. Wackernagel (1892) suggested that the $V/2$ constraint was only a special instance of what has come to be known as Wackernagel's Law: that the clitics, or unaccented words in a sentence, will be attracted into second position. In Sanskrit, the finite verb in principal clauses was indeed atonic, while the finite verb in subordinate clauses was not – a state of affairs that, if true for Indo-European dialects generally, would account for the position of the verb in German principal and subordinate clauses. A further study by the same writer (Wackernagel, 1898), established beyond serious question that the finite verb in Greek must also have been originally atonic.

The embarrassing fact remains that neither Greek nor Sanskrit, nor their progeny, ever became $V/2$ languages. The Germanic languages, on the other hand, for the accentuation of whose verbs we have no external evidence, did. Why?

By the same token, it is a mystery why of all the $V/2$ languages, it should have been exactly French and English which lost the target and became $V/3$ languages in surface structure.

If there are any general structural features or principles which determined these respective developments, they elude me.

4. Domains

As we lack independent criteria which would enable us to identify the languages that would become $V/2$ languages, so too we lack criteria to determine which sentence types in the given languages would become the DOMAIN for the $V/2$ target: in all the Germanic languages, this domain is simply the most neutral and unmarked form of the declarative principal clause. Why not the relative clause, or the interrogative?

Where do targets arise?

BIBLIOGRAPHY

Andrew, S. O.
1940 *Syntax and Style in Old English* (Cambridge University Press).
Andrews, A.
1971 "Case Agreement of Predicate Modifiers in Ancient Greek", *Linguist. Inquiry*, 2, 127-151.
Bach, E.
1961 "On Some Recurrent Types Of Transformations", in *Georgetown University Round Table: Selected Papers in Linguistics 1961-5*, ed. by R. J. O'Brien, S. J. (Georgetown University Press, 1968).
1962 "The Order of Elements in a Transformational Grammar of German", *Language*, 38, 263-269.
1971 "Questions", *Linguist. Inquiry*, 2, 153-166.
Bach, E. and R. Harms
1968 *Universals in Linguistic Theory* (New York, Holt).
Bech, G.
1952 *Über das niederländische Adverbialpronomen er*, T.C.L. de Copenhague 8 (Copenhagen, Nordisk Sprog og Kulturvorlag).
Bédier, J.
1924 *La Chanson de Roland* (Paris).
Beneš, E.
1962 "Die Verbstellung im Deutschen von der Mitteilungsperspektive her betrachtet", *Ph. Pragensia*, 5, 6-19.
Bierwisch, M., and K. Heidolph
1970 *Progress in Linguistics* (The Hague, Mouton).
Bernstein, E.
(n.d.) *The Order of Words in Old Norse Prose* (New York, The Knickerbocker Press).
Bolinger, D.
1961 "Syntactic Blends and Other Matters", *Language*, 37, 336-381.
Brunot, F.
1894 *Précis de l'Histoire de la Langue Française* (Paris, Masson).
1905 *Histoire de la Langue Française des Origines à 1900*, I (Paris, Armand Colin).
1906 the same, II.
1909 the same, III.
Carleton, C.
1971 *A Descriptive Syntax of the Old English Charters*, Janua Linguarum,

Series Practica 111 (The Hague, Mouton).

Cavigelli, P.
1969 *Die Germanisierung von Bonaduz* (Frauenfeld, Huber).

Chomsky, N.
1965 *Aspects of the Theory of Syntax* (Cambridge, M.I.T. Press).
1969 "Deep Structure, Surface Structure, and Semantic Interpretation", in Steinberg and Jakobovits (1971).

Curme, G.
1931 *Syntax*, III (Boston, Heath).

Dal, I.
1952 *Kurze deutsche Syntax* (Tübingen, Max Niemeyer).

Dauzat, A.
1930⁴ *Histoire de la Langue Française* (Paris, Payot).

Ebering, E.
1881 "Syntaktische Studien zu Froissart", *ZrPh*, 5, 323-376.

Einarsson, S.
1949 *Icelandic* (Johns Hopkins University Press).

Fillmore, C.
1968 "The Case for Case", in Bach and Harms (1968).

Garvin, P.
1963 "Linguistics in Czechoslovakia", in *Current Trends in Linguistics, I, Soviet and East European Linguistics* (The Hague, Mouton).

Gebhardt, C.
1896 "Zur subjektlosen Konstruktion im Altfranzösischen", *ZrPh*, 20, 27-50.

Greenberg, J.
1963 "Some Universals of Grammar with Particular Reference to the Order of Meaningful Constituents", in Greenberg (1963).

Greenberg, J., ed.
1963 *Universals of Language* (Cambridge, M.I.T. Press).

Grimm, J.
1898 *Deutsche Grammatik*, IV (Gütersloh, Bertelmann).

Haiman, J.
1971 "Targets and Paradigmatic Borrowing in Romantsch", *Language*, 47, 797-809.
1972 "Targets and Unmarked Structures", *Language*, 48, 365-377.

Hale, K.
1971 "Deep-Surface Canonical Disparities and Language Change: An Australian Case", unpublished mimeo, M.I.T.

Held, K.
1903 *Das Verbum ohne pronominales Subjekt im Althochdeutschen*, Palästra 31 (Berlin, Mayer und Müller).

Heusler, A.
1950 *Altisländisch* (Heidelberg, Carl Winter).

Hoenigswald, H.
1963 "Are There Universals of Linguistic Change?", in Greenberg (1963).

Horning, A.
1880 "Le Pronom neutre 'il' en Langue d'oil", *Rom. Stud.*, IV, 229-272.

Katz, J., and J. Fodor
1964   *The Structure of Language* (Englewood Cliffs, Prentice-Hall).
King, H.
1970   "On Blocking the Rules for Contraction in English", *Linguist. Inquiry*, 1, 134-136.
Kiparsky, P.
1965   "Phonological Change", unpublished doctoral dissertation, M.I.T.
1968   "Universals of Linguistic Change", in Bach and Harms (1968).
Kisseberth, C.
1970   "On the Functional Unity of Phonological Rules", *Linguist. Inquiry*, 1, 291-306.
Klima, E.
1964   "Negation in English", in Katz and Fodor (1964).
Kuno, S.
1971   "The Position of Locatives in Existential Sentences", *Linguist. Inquiry*, 2, 333-378.
Lakoff, G.
1969   "Generative Semantics", in Steinberg and Jakobovits (1971).
1970   "Global Rules", *Language*, 46, 627-639.
(ms.)   *Generative Semantics*.
Lakoff, G., and J. Ross
1966   "A Criterion for Verb Phrase Constituency", Harvard Computation Laboratory, Report to the National Science Foundation, 16.
Lees, R.
1960   "A Multiply Ambiguous Adjective Construction in English", *Language*, 36, 207-231.
Lerch, E.
1934   *Historische französische Syntax*, III (Leipzig, Reisland).
Lightner, T.
1968   "An Analysis of *Akan'e* and *Ikan'e* in Russian Using the Notion of Markedness", in *Studies Presented to Professor Roman Jakobson by his Students* (Cambridge, Slavia Publishers).
Lockwood, W.
1964²   *An Introduction to Modern Faroese* (København, Munksgaard).
1969   *Historical German Syntax* (Oxford, Clarendon Press).
Maetzner, A.
1874   *An English Grammar*, tr. by C. Grece (London, J. Murray).
Maurer, F.
1926   *Untersuchungen über die deutsche Verbalstellung in ihrer geschichtlichen Entwicklung* (Heidelberg, Carl Winter).
McCawley, J.
1970   "English as a VSO Language", *Language*, 46, 286-299.
Miklosich, F.
1883   *Subjektlose Sätze* (Wien, Bräumüller).
Morf, H.
1878   "Die Wortstellung im altfranzösischen Rolandslied", *Rom. Stud.*, III, 199-294.

Paul, H.
1919 *Deutsche Grammatik*, III (Tübingen, Max Niemeyer).
Perlmutter, D.
1968 "Deep and Surface Structure Constraints in Syntax", unpublished doctoral dissertation, M.I.T.
1970 "On the Article in English", in Bierwisch and Heidolph (1970).
1971 *Deep and Surface Structure Constraints in Syntax* (New York, Holt).
Peters, S.
1970 "Why there are Many 'Universal Bases'", *P.I.L.*, 2, 27-44.
Peters S., and R. Ritchie
1969 "A Note on the Universal Base Hypothesis", *J. Linguist.*, 5, 151-152.
Pogatscher, A.
1901 "Unausgedrücktes Subjekt im Altenglischen", *Anglia*, 23, 261-301.
Rosenbaum, P.
1967 *The Grammar of English Predicate Complement Constructions*, Research Monograph 47 (Cambridge M.I.T. Press).
Ross, J.
1967 "Constraints on Variables in Syntax", unpublished doctoral dissertation, M.I.T.
1969a "A Proposed Rule of Tree Pruning", in Reibel and Schane (1969).
1969b "Auxiliaries as Main Verbs", *Studies in Philosophical Linguistics*, I, 77-102.
1970a "Gapping and the Order of Constituents", in Schane and Reibel (1970).
1970b "Leftward Ho!", unpublished mimeo, M.I.T.
Schane, S., and D. Reibel
1969 *Modern Studies in English-Readings in Transformational Grammar* (Englewood Cliffs, Prentice-Hall).
Schlickum, J.
1882 "Die Wortstellung in der altfranzösischen Dichtung Aucassin und Nicolette", *Fr. Stud.*, 3, 177-222.
Smith, C.
1893 "The Order of Words in Anglo-Saxon Prose", *Publications of the M.L.A.*, New Series, I, 210-244.
Smyth, G.
1956 *Greek Grammar*, revised by G. Messing (Cambridge, Harvard University Press).
Spies, H.
1901 *Studien zur Geschichte des englischen Pronomens im 15. und 16. Jahrhundert*, Studien zur englischen Philologie 1 (Halle, Max Niemeyer).
Steblin-Kamensky, I.
1955 *Drevneislandski Jazyk* (Moskva-Leningrad, Izdatel'stvo na Inostrannyx Jazykax).
Steinberg, D., and L. Jakobovits
1971 *Semantics – An Interdisciplinary Reader* (Cambridge University Press).
Streitberg, E.
1906² *Gotisches Elementarbuch* (Heidelberg, Carl Winter).

Suchier, H.
1909 *Aucassin et Nicolette*, Texte critique par H. Suchier, traduction française par A. Conson (Paderborn).
Swieczkowski, W.
1962 *Word Order Patterning in Middle English*, Janua Linguarum 19 (The Hague, Mouton).
Szamosi, M.
1970 "A Surface Structure Constraint in Hungarian", unpublished mimeo, Language Research Foundation.
Thurneysen, R.
1892 "Zur Stellung des Verbums in Altfranzösischen", *ZrPh.*, 16, 289-307.
Wackernagel, J.
1892 "Ueber ein Gesetz der indogermanischen Wortstellung", *Indo-german. Forsch.*, 1, 333-436.
1898 "Der griechische Verbalaccent", *K.Z.*, 23, 457-470.
Wackernagel, W.
1835 *Altdeutsches Lesebuch* (Berne, Schweigheuser).
Wahlén, N.
1925 *The Old English Impersonalia* (Göteborg, Elanders).
Walther von der Vogelweide
1955 *Sprüche; Der Leich; Lieder*, Urtext mit Uebertragung von P. Stapf (Berlin-Darmstadt, Tempel).
Weinrich, U.
1953 *Languages in Contact* (Columbia University Press).
Wessén, E.
1970 *Schwedische Sprachgeschichte*, III, Grundriss der germanischen Philologie 183 (Berlin, Walter de Gruyter).
Wilmanns, W.
1906 *Deutsche Grammatik*, III (Strassburg, Tübner).
Wright, J.
1954[2] *Grammar of the Gothic Language* (Oxford University Press).

INDEX